DYNAMIC STUDIES
IN 1 PETER & 2 PETER

BRINGING GOD'S WORD TO LIFE

FRED A. SCHEEREN

WESTBOW
PRESS®
A DIVISION OF THOMAS NELSON
& ZONDERVAN

WestBow Press books may be ordered through booksellers or by contacting:

WestBow Press
A Division of Thomas Nelson & Zondervan
1663 Liberty Drive
Bloomington, IN 47403
www.westbowpress.com
1 (866) 928-1240

ISBN: 978-1-9736-6461-1 (sc)
ISBN: 978-1-9736-6460-4 (e)

Library of Congress Control Number: 2019906478

Print information available on the last page.

WestBow Press rev. date: 07/18/2019

DEDICATION

I DEDICATE THIS book to my lovely wife, Sally, who is a Jewish believer and Ivy League educated attorney. She has stood by me over the years and raised our sons in our God-loving home. The comfort of sharing our friendship and our love for Christ has encouraged me greatly in creating this series of dynamic studies of various books of the Bible. Sally's participation in our small group studies has added a much deeper dimension of richness to the discussions. Thank you for sharing your heritage, training, and knowledge.

CONTENTS

ACKNOWLEDGMENTS

MY FRIEND, BOB Mason, who at the time I began the Dynamic Bible Studies series was in his second career as the pastor of small groups at the Bible Chapel in the South Hills of Pittsburgh, suggested the overall structure of each study. Realizing our group was doing more in-depth work than most, he asked that I include several important segments in each lesson—most specifically, the warm-up and life application phases.

Bob suggested a great resource called the *New Testament Lesson Planner* from InterVarsity Press. I have augmented this with commentaries by Dr. Charles Missler from Koinonia House, the *Wiersbe Bible Commentary*, *The MacArthur Bible Handbook* by Dr. John MacArthur, the *Bible Commentaries* of J. Vernon McGee, and the whole of Scripture itself. To make the utilization of the whole of Scripture more efficient, I have also leaned heavily on the Libronix Digital Library, perhaps the most advanced Bible software available, and other resources to help us understand how the New Testament and the Tanakh (Old Testament) fit together as one cohesive document.

I have also enjoyed the input and encouragement of my friend, Ron Jones, as I have continued to prepare these studies. Ron is a former high school principal and administrator. He is also a committed believer and daily student of God's Word. His background in education coupled with his love of God and His Word has made him a powerful force for good.

I would like to express thanks to my good friend, Gordon Haresign, for his continued support and encouragement in my efforts to produce the Dynamic Bible Studies series. Gordon's journey began with his birth in the Belgian Congo. In the following years he was a senior executive with an international accounting firm, served in the military, labored as a Bible college professor, was instrumental in the leadership of a worldwide Bible correspondence school, and currently serves as the Chairman of the Board of Directors of Scripture Union, an international Bible-based ministry. Gordon's work as a teacher, speaker, and missionary has taken him to over 50 countries on five continents. His two most recent books, *Authentic Christianity* and *Pray for the Fire to Fall* should be required reading for all believers. Speaking of the Dynamic Bible Studies series he has written, "These are among the finest, if not the finest, inductive Bible studies available today. I strongly endorse them."

I would also like to express my appreciation to my two proof-readers. This includes:

- Cynthia Nicastro, an intelligent, ardent and devoted student of the Scriptures and a meticulous grammarian.

- My wife Sally, a Jewish believer and Ivy League educated lawyer who was law review in law school, worked for the Superior Court of the State of Pennsylvania, and is now in private practice.

May God bless you, inspire you, teach you, and change your life for the better as you work through these lessons.

PREFACE

Welcome to what I hope you find to be a most enjoyable and enlightening study of two letters written by one of the most courageous and influential men in history. This man's life was changed from that of a boisterous, fearless, impetuous ruffian to one of the most dedicated followers of the Jewish Messiah. These letters are part of the group of documents that today is known as "The Bible" and are referred to as the Books of First and Second Peter.

As we consider how these books of the Bible fit into the whole of the New Testament and the Tanakh (the name used by Jews for the Old Testament, used here to emphasize the Jewishness of the Scriptures), we need to realize a number of things. We should stand in awe of this collection of 66 books, written over thousands of years by at least 40 different authors. Every detail of the text is there by design. It explains history before it happens, and comes to us from outside the dimension of time. It is, in short, the most amazing, most authenticated, and most accurate book available in the world.

If this claim is not strong enough, add to it the indisputable fact that the words contained therein have changed more lives than any others now in existence.

While the Judeo-Christian Scriptures are demonstrably perfect, my prepared studies are not. There is no way I or anyone else could possibly incorporate the depth of the text into individual sessions. I simply desire to provide a vehicle for others to use in their investigation of the Scriptures as they incorporate these timeless truths into their lives.

Speaking of small groups, Dr. Chuck Missler, a former Fortune 500 CEO, said, "I experienced more growth in my personal life as a believer by participating in small group Bible studies than anything else." I believe you may find this to be true in your experience and encourage you to be an active participant in such a mutually supportive, biblically-based group.

GROUND RULES

I DESIGNED THE first portion of each study to encourage readers to think about their personal situation. I designed the second portion to help people understand what the text says and how it relates to the whole of Scripture. And finally, each lesson ends with a discussion designed to help people apply that lesson.

You will notice that, in most instances, I have included the citation, but not the actual text of the Scripture we are considering. I did this on purpose. I believe we all learn more effectively if we have to dig out the text itself. As a byproduct of that exercise, we become more familiar with this marvelous book.

Scripture references are preceded or followed by a question or series of questions. Again, this is on purpose. I have also found that people seem to learn most effectively when employing the Socratic Method. That is, instead of telling someone what the text says and how it relates to other texts and life, they will remember it better if they answer questions about it and ferret out the information for themselves.

In a few instances, I have inserted additional commentary or partial answers to some of the questions to help the group get the most out of the study.

It is my intention and suggestion that the various scripture references be read out loud as part of each session. Shorter passages might be read by one participant, while anything over two or three verses might serve everyone better if one member reads one verse and another reads the next until the passage is completed. This keeps everyone involved. After reading these passages, I intend that how they relate to the primary Scripture at hand in Colossians or Philemon be seriously considered. At times, this relationship seems to be available and obvious on the surface. In many other instances, the interconnectedness of the whole of Scripture and its principles are most effectively understood through deeper thought, discussion, and prayer.

In commenting on and discussing the various passages, questions, concepts, and principles in this material, it is not required that any particular person give his or her input. The reader of any passage may, but is not pressured to, give his or her thoughts to the group. This is a group participation exercise for the mutual benefit of all involved and many people in the group giving their insight into a certain verse or question will often enhance the learning experience.

I also have two practical suggestions if you work through this book in a small group setting. Every time you meet, I suggest you review the calendar and agree upon the next scheduled meeting as well as who will bring refreshments. This will help the group to run a lot more smoothly while enhancing everyone's enjoyment, experience, and expectations.

INTRODUCTION TO THE LETTERS OF PETER

We are now about to examine the books of the Bible known as 1 and 2 Peter. Not surprisingly, they were penned by Peter, arguably the most famous and well-known disciple of Jesus of Nazareth, also known as the Jewish Messiah or Jesus Christ.

So just who was Peter?

He was a burly fisherman who operated on the lake of Galilee in Israel during the time it was under Roman occupation. He hailed from Beth-saida, a city of considerable Greek influence, but also had a home in the town of Capernaum which was in the region of Galilee. The book of Mark indicates that he retained the accent of people from the town where he was born and raised. His life seems to have been impacted by the movement of John the Baptist. This interest in the things spoken of by John culminated in Peter being introduced to Jesus by his brother, Andrew. The introduction resulted in Peter making the life altering decision to follow the man he came to know as Yeshua Hamaschiach, the long-awaited Jewish Messiah.

He made his decision in response to Jesus choosing him. Jesus, in fact, gave Peter a new title. He called him *Kephas* (Aramaic), which is normally translated *Cephas* in English, and appears as *Petros* in the Greek language. This new approbation means "rock" or "stone" and was an apt description not only of who Peter was when he met Jesus, but who he would become.

When mention is made of the disciples of Jesus, Peter always stands first among them. He was a man of extreme boldness and bravery. Indeed, when over six hundred battle hardened soldiers came to arrest and execute Jesus Peter acted in the bold fashion for which he was known. He took the only action that came naturally to him, which did not even cross the minds of anyone else in Jesus' party. Peter drew his sword and attacked this mob of fighting men with battle lust in his heart and the readiness to immediately overthrow the yoke of their Roman oppressors.

However, Peter became confused when Jesus not only stopped his attack, but healed the man Peter stuck with his sword. This led to his befuddlement and famous denials of his association with Jesus, just as Jesus Himself had predicted. And, just as Jesus also predicted, this led to Peter coming back into the fold and becoming the leader of the "church" in Jerusalem in hostile territory.

As the de-facto leader of the believers in Jerusalem, Peter took the lead as their spokesman before the Jewish authorities. He became the first apostle to give assent to taking the Good News of Life to Gentiles after his denouncement by Paul for not having done so. Obviously, Peter had learned to heed God's leading despite his human tendency toward the predilection to ram on ahead with little thought. His relationship with Jesus and the power of the Holy Spirit made him a changed man.

Peter formed a powerful team in Jerusalem with John, another one of Jesus' apostles. As his experience and work grew so did his influence as he became the leader of the early church. In this role he was imprisoned but miraculously escaped. From there he traveled throughout the region and in fact much of the known world, encouraging, teaching and giving aid to believers as he went. He ultimately ended up in Rome, where he was imprisoned and so far as we can tell was crucified upside down, not believing he was worthy to be put to death in the same manner as his Lord.

Peter's first letter appears to have been written from Rome (1 Peter 5:13) either just before or during the early part of the persecutions of the deranged Roman Emperor, Nero. Interestingly, besides burning Rome and blaming it on the followers of the Jewish Messiah, Nero appears to have been involved with the execution of the apostle Paul and is widely thought to have been the primary mover in Peter's execution as well.

WEEK 1

GOD'S PROMISE FULFILLED
1 PETER 1:1-12

Open in Prayer

Group Warm-Up Question

What is something you once searched for very hard?

Read: 1 Peter 1:1-12

Reread: 1 Peter 1:1

To whom did Peter address this letter?

Where were these people living?

Why do you think he said these people were "living as foreigners"? After all, they were living in what had become their "home towns."

Note 1: This had a special meaning to Jewish believers. The Greek word used is *diasporas*. Going forward, the diaspora referred to Jews who were separated from their homeland in Israel.

Note 2: The Greek translated as *foreigners* or *strangers in this world*, depending upon which translation of the Bible you are using, literally means "temporary residents" or "refugees."

Note 3: Larry Norman, the "Father of Christian Rock," had a keen sense of this. Indeed, in his most famous album entitled *Only Visiting This Planet*, he quips "This world is not my home. I'm just passin' through." Interestingly, this particular album, released in 1972, was voted the greatest Christian album ever recorded by CCM magazine in 1990. By the year 2001, 29 years after its release, it had fallen to second place. In 2014 it was announced as the first Christian rock album chosen for the Library of Congress National Recording Registry. This majestic, complex, intensely professional work is still available from Solid Rock Records on CD and most certainly through electronic media.

Read the following verses for more insight on this subject and jot down what you observe:

1 Chronicles 29:15

Hebrews 11:13-16

John 15:19

John 17:14-17

1 John 2:15

James 1:27

James 4:4

Romans 12:2

1 Peter 2:11-12

Philippians 3:20

When do you feel as if you are a stranger in this world?

Do non-believers ever feel this way about you? Please explain.

Is this a good thing? Please read the following verses as you construct your answer.

Philippians 2:14-16

Matthew 5:11-16

Reread: 1 Peter 1:2

When did Peter say the believers he was writing to were "chosen" by God?

Since Peter mentions the important concept of being chosen at the outset we ought to take the time to deal with it and what it means in actual practice.

Read: Ephesians 1:4

What did God do before the world was created?

What did God intend to be the result of His action?

In his book *Evangelism and the Sovereignty of God*, J. I. Packer states that the sovereignty of God and man's responsibility is an antinomy--an appearance of contradiction between conclusions which seem equally logical, reasonable or necessary (p. 18). He continues to say that while God "orders and controls all things, human actions among them . . . He holds every man responsible for the choices he makes and the courses of action he pursues" (p.22).

Read: John 6:36-40

What promise do we see for those who come to trust in Jesus?

How did Jesus summarize His Father's will?

Note: This passage contains some concepts that are sometimes, on the surface, difficult for those of us with finite minds to understand. We see:

1. God's promise to those who come to Jesus.

2. The concept that one must come to Jesus to receive life.

3. The statements about those who have come to Him and are going to come to Him. (He already knows.)

4. The statement that the Lord wants all men and women to come to Him.

This seeming conundrum can be more fully understood as one studies the Scriptures and views them a whole. In other words:

1. God wants all people to come to Him.

2. We must choose to come to Him.

3. The "elect" will come to Him.

4. God knows who will come to Him.

We can see this borne out in the following verses:

John 17:2

John 17:6

John 17:9

John 17:11-12

John 17:24

2 Thessalonians 2:13

1 Timothy 2:3-4

Luke 19:10

2 Peter 3:9

We also see that God makes a bona fide offer to every person in the following verses:

John 3:16

John 3:36

John 5:24

Romans 10:9

Romans 10:13

We see the concept of this antinomy working in John 6:37 where we find that all who come are received and all who are given come.

Some people find it helpful to think of this in terms of a "life parade." Imagine God, who is not bound by the constraints of time, flying high in a helicopter above a parade of the events that will make up your life. He knows the beginning from the end, He knows the way He wants you to go, and yet you have a choice.

Does this concept seem difficult to understand? No wonder.

See:

- Isaiah 55:8-9

- Ephesians 3:18

Read: Ephesians 1:5

What did God decide in advance for those who come to Him by trusting in Yeshua Hamaschiah, the Jewish Messiah, who we know as Jesus?

Let's take a moment and further attempt to make two words about the future, God's foreknowledge and their meaning more clear, drawing upon insights from Warren Wiersbe.

1. The first word is "predestination." As this word is used in the Bible it refers primarily to what God does and will do for people who have come to know Him through a personal relationship with Jesus Christ. <u>Nowhere in the Judeo Christian Scriptures does it indicate that anyone is predestined to hell. The word is used only in relationship to God's people.</u> For example, God's purpose for history and believers as He has already decided relates to:

   - The crucifixion (Acts 4:25-28).

- Our adoption into the family of God (Ephesians 1:5).

- Our conformity to Jesus (Romans 8:29-30).

- Our future inheritance (Ephesians 1:11).

2. The second word is "election," which refers to people, their choices and God's foreknowledge as already discussed.

What made the believers to whom Peter was writing "holy"?

How do you see this working in actual practice?

Read the following verses for insight into this question:

Romans 8:9

Ephesians 1:13-14

Galatians 5:19-21

Galatians 5:22-23

2 Corinthians 5:17

Exodus 24:7

Romans 1:5

Romans 15:18

What example of this have you seen in your own life?

What are the real and expected results of having been made holy in this fashion as seen in 1 Peter 1:2? Please list them and describe what they mean to you.

1.

2.

What was Peter's wish for the believers who were victoriously participating in a new life following Jesus Christ?

Reread: 1 Peter 1:3

Also Read: 2 Corinthians 1:3

To whom does all honor actually belong?

What great privilege has God extended to those who trust Jesus?

What in God's character enables Him to extend this privilege to people?

Do we deserve this privilege? Please read the following verses as you put together your answer.

Romans 3:23

Romans 6:23

Ephesians 2:8-9

What makes it possible, besides the character of God, for us to take advantage of this privilege?

Read the following verses as you put together your answer:

1 Peter 1:23

John 3:1-21

How should believers live and think as a result of having this privilege?

Read: John 16:33

Is this peace available to all believers?

What two prerequisites do you see in the sentence preceding the last one in 1 Peter 1:2 as they relate to this peace?

Reread: 1 Peter 1:4

What has God reserved for His children?

Who are these children for whom God reserved this incomparable gift? Please read the following verses as you construct your answer.

John 3:3

John 1:12

1 John 3:7-10

Where is God keeping this special thing?

In what condition is God keeping this for believers? Please list the characteristics of this condition and jot down what this means to you.

1.

2.

3.

4.

Note: The same word used for this future inheritance is used to refer to Israel's promised possession of the land in Joshua 11:23.

What parallels can you draw between the special inheritance of believers and Israel's possession of the land?

1 Peter 1:5

What does God promise to do prior to a believer actually receiving what He is keeping for them?

For how long does God promise to do this?

According to this verse, why is He doing this?

By what means is God doing this? We see two listed.

1.

2.

Read: Philippians 4:7

Note: The Greek word used in 1 Peter 1:5 and Philippians 4:7 indicating that believers are protected by God's power is *phrouroumenous*. This is a military term that means:

- To guard.

- To prevent hostile invasion.

- To keep the inhabitants of a besieged city from having to take flight.

What further insight to you gain from this understanding of the original language?

What part do we have in seeing this promise come to pass in our lives?

When will what God is keeping for believers be fully revealed to them?

Obviously, this verse does not indicate that believers will not encounter trials or difficulty in life. If it doesn't mean that, what do you think it means?

Reread: 1 Peter 1:6

What is ahead for believers when they receive what God is keeping for them?

What must believers endure prior to the time they receive this great gift?

What do you take this to mean?

What trials have you faced in the past?

What trials are you facing now?

Read: 1 John 5:4

How might one summarize the way in which believers ultimately experience victory?

Reread: 1 Peter 1:7

Why are believers subject to trials? According to this verse there are at least four reasons. Please list them.

1.

2.

3.

4.

How precious is a person's faith, their trust in God, to Him?

Please explain your vision of this?

Why do you think our faith is so precious to God?

Why is it important that one's faith remain strong after being tested by fiery trials?

If one's faith has been tested and refined, what is the ultimate result? What will it bring to the believer? Again, please make a list.

1.

2.

3.

When will these things come to fruition?

Read: James 1:2

Why might one find joy in the midst of trials, or even because of trials? Please make a list.

    1.

    2.

    3.

    4.

    5.

    6.

    7.

According to this verse, what do trials show about one's faith?

How and why do you think this happens?

In the world today what form might the fiery trials referenced in this verse take? Please jot down several below.

    1.

    2.

    3.

4.

5.

6.

Note: The verse we are considering indicates that there is a difference between one's faith being refined and one's faith being strengthened.

Refining is a term usually used of a <u>natural resource</u> that is almost in a usable form, but which is <u>more useful</u> in its pure form.

Strengthening is generally described as the process of making something stronger or <u>more effective.</u>

How have the trials you have experienced refined your faith?

How have the trials you have endured strengthened your faith?

How do these two concepts work together?

What has been the result of this refining and strengthening in your life?

Reread: 1 Peter 1:8

Also read: John 20:29

Peter and John mention a number of things endemic to the relationship the believers to whom he was writing had with Jesus Christ, even though these particular people had not seen Him in person. What are they?

1.

2.

3.

4.

5.

Breaking down the last portion of this verse further, what do you think it means to be "happy with a glorious, inexpressible joy"?

How is it possible for this to be the case when one is in the midst of the fiery trials Peter has already mentioned?

How does this apply to the life of a believer today?

Have you experienced the joy mentioned in this verse? Please explain.

Is this joy available to all believers?

What must one do to appropriate it?

For more insight on joy read Philippians 4:4.

Some people find it to be a stark realization when they come to understand that the Scriptures indicate that experiencing joy is a choice.

The Merriam Webster dictionary defines joy as "the emotion evoked by well-being, success, or good fortune or by the prospect of possessing what one desires."

This joy comes from within a person and can be kindled or extinguished based upon what is happening in the heart, mind, and spirit of someone.

While happiness is somewhat related, the feeling of contentment and well-being associated with it is based upon external circumstances alone and one's response to them.

Strangely, then, it is possible for a person to be joyful without being happy or happy without being joyful.

Knowing that joy is a choice, how do people in the world today attempt to achieve joy on their own?

Read:

1Thessalonians 5:16-22

Galatians 5:22-23.

2 Timothy 3:16-17

According to these verses, in what way can a believer experience true joy in the midst of the trials and tribulations of life?

Reread: 1 Peter 1:9

What is the primary reward one receives for placing their trust in Jesus Christ?

Reread: 1 Peter 1:10

What was it that the prophets wanted to know more about?

1 Peter 1:11

What did the prophets predict?

By what power were the prophets able to do this?

For examples of this please read:

Isaiah 50:6 (Written about 700 years before the birth of Jesus Christ.)

Isaiah 52:13 through Isaiah 53

Psalm 22 (Written 500-1,000 years before the birth of Jesus.)

Note: There are over 300 prophecies in the Old Testament, which the Jews call the Tanakh, about the first coming of Jesus Christ. They were all fulfilled to the letter in the Jewish Messiah. It is mathematically impossible for this to have happened by chance.

For more on this topic I suggest that two members if your group provide brief reports on the following items at a future meeting.

1. Composite Probability in the Appendices of this book.

2. *100 Prophecies fulfilled by Jesus* from Rose Publishing.

Reread: 1 Peter 1:12

When did the prophets understand that the things they were writing about would come to pass?

By what power did they understand this future fact of history?

How is this same power involved in the transmission of the Good News today? Please explain.

Read: Ephesians 3:10

Note: The mention of the church in this verse refers to all people everywhere who have trusted Jesus Christ on a personal basis.

Read:

Luke 15:10

Luke 15:7

What are the angels doing as the Good News is shared in the world today?

Application Questions

What is your attitude toward the trials in your life?

According to what we studied today, does it need to be adjusted? How so?

Close in Prayer

WEEK 2

PREPARE FOR ACTION
1 PETER 1:13-2:3

Open in Prayer

Before getting into the meat of today's study I suggest we listen to the two reports assigned at the last meeting on:

3. Composite Probability in the Appendices of this book.

4. *100 Prophecies Fulfilled by Jesus* from Rose Publishing.

Group Warm-Up Questions

What standards or examples do many people use to determine how they should live?

When was the last time you felt like a stranger?

Read: 1 Peter 1:13-2:3

Reread: 1 Peter 1:13

What three imperatives for believers do we find in this verse? Please list them in the order presented.

1.

2.

3.

Might these three operate not only in concert, but in harmonious succession? That is, might they build upon each other as they are exercised in order and put into practice? Please explain how this might work.

Note: The Greek word translated as "be sober" or "self-controlled," depending upon which translation of the Bible you are using, means to be free from every form of mental and spiritual "drunkenness" or excess.

What additional insight does this knowledge of the original language give you into these imperatives?

Note: Chuck Missler pointed out that by this time in the first chapter of Peter the return of Jesus Christ had already been referenced four times. (See 1 Peter 1:5, 7, 9, 13.) What does this tell us about the importance of this future event?

Why do you think it is that so many people today give this future event such little thought?

With Peter and the early believers as our example, how should we regard it?

Reread: 1 Peter 1:14

What additional positive command are believers to follow?

What does this mean to you?

What must believers avoid?

What excuse might some people have had for poor behavior prior to trusting Jesus Christ on a personal basis?

What excuse do they have now?

Do they, in fact, have any valid excuse at all?

When are people tempted by evil desires?

Why is it necessary for the three imperatives mentioned in 1 Peter 1:13 to be operant in one's life for a believer to successfully fulfil the command in 1 Peter 1:14?

Reread: 1 Peter 1:15-16

Also Read:

Leviticus 11:44-45

Leviticus 19:2

Leviticus 20:7

Reread: 1 Peter 1:17

What one thing in particular does Peter admonish us to remember about our heavenly father?

How will God judge and reward believers?

Knowing this, how shall we live during our time on earth?

Note: Reading this verse you might remember that the Bible tells us that Israel is the "Apple of God's eye," and that the Jews are His chosen people. Indeed, He has used the Jewish people and the nation of Israel throughout history for the transmission of His Word and, according to the Scriptures, will continue to use them. However, as this one verse, written by the Jewish leader of the early believers reminds us, we must all give account and will be held responsible for our behavior whether we are Gentiles or Jews.

In your own words, what does it mean to be "holy."

The Merriam Webster dictionary defines holy as an adjective that means "exalted or worthy of complete devotion as one perfect in goodness and righteousness."

How do you see yourself measuring up?

Reread: 1 Peter 1:18-19

How does Peter describe the life we inherited from our ancestors?

How was our ransom paid?

How does Peter describe Jesus Christ in these verses?

Note: At the time, Peter was writing to many Jewish believers as well as Gentiles. He was telling them that their old religious practices, while quite extensive and meaningful, had no value apart from the Messiah. Indeed, the Jewish believers, who had a clear understanding of the Tanakh (what the Jews called the Old Testament), realized that Jesus Himself was the prophetic fulfillment of the Passover Feast they had been celebrating for over one thousand five hundred years.

You may, perhaps at your leisure, also wish to read Exodus 12 for more information about the Passover.

Read the following verses and jot down what we learn from them.

John 1:29

Hebrews 9:14

Reread: 1 Peter 1:20

When did God make the decision to use His own Son as a ransom for us?

When was this finally revealed so that it was clear for anyone to see it with only a little bit of scholarship? Why?

Read: 1 Peter 1:21

What three facets of one's relationship with God can become a reality through Christ?

    1.

    2.

    3.

According to this verse, what acts of God make this all work?

    1.

    2.

Why do you think these two particular acts of God are so important?

Reread: I Peter 1:22

Also Read: Psalm 119:9

What do you think it means when Peter says these people "obeyed the truth?" Please explain.

What happened to these people when they "obeyed the truth?"

What does Peter say believers should be doing as a result of this cleansing?

Peter also mentions three aspects of the resultant love that God desires. Please list them.

1.

2.

3.

Why is it of such importance that this love be:

Sincere as for brothers and sisters?

Deep?

Experienced with all of one's heart?

Note: This type of love, which in the Greek appears as *Agape*, refers to the self-sacrificial type of deep love that might cause a person to lay down their life to save another person. It can only come from a changed heart.

Reread: 1 Peter 1:23

With what term does Peter summarize what has happened to these people?

Having had this experience, when does it end?

How long does it last?

Where does this new life come from?

What particular words does Peter use to describe the Word of God?

    1.

    2.

Reread: 1 Peter 1:24-25

Also read: Isaiah 40:6-8

How does the Scripture describe the earthly lives of people?

How is the Word of God described?

What is contained in the eternal Word of God?

Note: Scripture, speaking of itself, is replete with descriptions and admonitions regarding the "Word of God." Read the following excerpts and jot down what you see.

Psalm 19:7-11

Psalm 111:7-8

Psalm 112:1

Psalm 119

Hebrews 4:12

2 Timothy 3:16-17

Knowing the importance of God's Word, why do some religious people neglect it today?

What impact does it have upon a person when they neglect God's Word?

What positive impact does it have upon a person, a family, an organization, or a nation that heeds the Word of God?

Please discuss an example of the peril into which a person, nation or organization has fallen by neglecting the Word of God when it was available to them.

Conversely, please discuss an example of the power unleashed when a person, organization or nation heeds God's Word.

Reread: 1 Peter 2:1

What things in particular does Peter say believers should be rid of? Please make a list. (This list is sometimes referred to as "Five Sins of Attitude and Speech.")

1.

2.

3.

4.

5.

Note: In some translations of the Bible this list has been contracted into a list of four to improve the readability in English. However, in order to be true to the original text I believe it behooves us to take a look at each of the components in the original language. If we look to the Greek we will find it is comprised of:

1. *Kadian*, which we generally think of as malice. It involves a desire to inflict harm, pain or injury on another person and is sometimes called wicked ill-will.

2. *Dolon*, which we generally think of as dishonesty. It involves deliberate slander, treachery, lies, negative craftiness and sneakiness, guile and deceit. God hates lies and lumps that particular sin in with others that seem worse to some in the modern world. (See Revelation 21:8.)

3. *Hypokriseis,* which we often simply call hypocrisy. However, this is more far-reaching than most people imagine. It is no accident of action or speech. It involves deliberate pretended piety and love. It is pretending to be what one is not. God hates all dishonesty and in particular hypocrisy. (See Matthew 15:7-8 and Isaiah 29:13.)

4. *Phthonous,* which we think of as envy. It involves resentful discontent for what one has and a hateful scheming desire for what others possess.

5. *Katalalias,* which we generally think of as slander. This involves saying things about others that one knows are not true. Some people think of it as backbiting lies.

The fact that Peter mentions these specific things in particular further makes at least three inferences.

1. These practices must be particularly destructive to:

   - A person's life.

   - A person's witness.

   - A person's influence upon the groups in which they are involved.

   - All groups of believers.

2. They must have been evident in some of the believers at that time.

3. Since they are included in God's Word the directives against them are focused not just upon the people receiving Peter's letter at that time. They are directed toward all believers throughout time.

Looking at the list above, why do you think these particular things are so destructive?

Chuck Missler felt that gossip was the most personally hurtful of all sins of this type and cited it as a violation of Exodus 20:16. What do you think and why?

Reread: 1 Peter 2:2

What does Peter tell these believers that they must crave?

What is to be the result of taking advantage of this resource?

In case there is any doubt, what is the resource that Peter is talking about?

Clue: He just spoke about it in 1 Peter 1:25.

How can a believer expect to grow, be pleasing to God, and enjoy the benefits of a relationship through Jesus Christ if not taking advantage of the precious resource He has made available?

How badly does Peter say that believers should desire the nourishment available through the Word of God?

Suggested Activity:

Assume that you are a great student of a certain activity and fan of a person who is the best at what they do. Pick your activity and personage.

Now assume that this person is coming to your locale in a month.

Let us further assume that you have somehow been able to arrange to share a one-on-one meal with this person for one hour.

Note: At this point I suggest that everyone in the group stop and name the particular person with whom they would enjoy sharing dinner and discussion.

Going one step further, let us also assume that this person has written a best-selling book with 66 chapters that is hundreds of pages long in which they detail the secrets of their success.

In preparation for your upcoming dinner conversation with this special person, what would you do to prepare for your interaction with them over the course of the next month? Why?

Realizing that every human being will someday meet God, and that He has indeed made "His book" available to us, what should every person do?

Even if someone does not choose to believe that there is a God, what should they do on the chance that they are wrong?

I realize it is a mathematical and scientific impossibility that one who has trusted Jesus Christ and studied the Word of God is wrong about the principles in the

Scriptures and a life lived in concert with them is incorrect. However, what might such a person loose at the point of death if they are wrong?

Conversely, consider a person who has rejected God, His Son as revealed in the Scriptures, and His Word and finds at the point of death that they are wrong. What have they lost?

Application Questions

As you understand it, what personal characteristics or tendencies do you need to be rid of in your life to become more the person God intends?

How can you tangibly show your love for other believers this week?

Close in Prayer

THE LIVING STONE AND LIVING THE FAITH
1 PETER 2:4-12

Open in Prayer

Group Warm-Up Questions

What is your ethnic heritage and how has it influenced you?

When is a time you have been rejected when offering to assist someone in a way that would have been quite helpful to them?

Read: 1 Peter 2:4-12

Reread: 1 Peter 2:4

Who is the living cornerstone of God's temple?

What is the difference between how God treated the living Cornerstone and how people in general treated Him?

Important Note: Various theologians have wrangled with the meaning of Matthew 16:13-17. However, as we can clearly see in 1 Peter 2:4, Peter himself understood that the "church" was to be built on Jesus Christ and His identity. Peter was certainly a leader, but the Cornerstone was and is the Jewish Messiah, the very Son of the living God. He ties this together by speaking of:

1. A living hope.

    • See 1 Peter 1:3.

2. The living Word.

    • See 1 Peter 1:23.

3. The living stone.

    • See 1 Peter 2:4.

Reread: 1 Peter 2:5

In what way are believers like "living stones?"

What other privileges and functions do believers enjoy besides that of being "living stones?"

Note 1: We see believers as a whole making up the church referred to in:

- 1 Corinthians 3:16

- Ephesians 2:21

- Ephesians 2:22

Note 2: We also see believers referred to as a "holy priesthood" and offering "spiritual sacrifices" in:

- 1 Peter 2:9

- Hebrews 4:16

- Revelation 1:6

And we see that we need no mediator other than Jesus Christ to approach God directly in:

- 1 Timothy 2:5

Reread: 1 Peter 2:5

Also read:

1 Peter 1:16

1 Peter 1:22

Hebrews 13:15

Romans 1:1-2

What do you think Peter is referring to when he says that believers offer "spiritual sacrifices that please God?"

Reread: 1 Peter 2:6

Also read: Isaiah 28:16

Where is God placing the "Cornerstone?"

What do you think is the significance of this placement?

For what is this Cornerstone chosen?

What is the fate of those who trust in the Cornerstone?

Looking at the prophecy in Isaiah in concert with the 1 Peter 2:6, what are the words used to describe the Cornerstone? Please make a list.

    1.

    2.

    3.

    4.

    5.

These two verses also list several things that will not happen to those who trust in the Cornerstone. What are they? Please make another list using the various translations of the Bible available to you.

    1.

    2.

    3.

4.

5.

What do you think it means that those who trust in the Cornerstone will never experience these things?

Reread: 1 Peter 2:7

Also Read:

Psalm 118:22

Matthew 21:42

Matthew 21:44

What do those who have come to trust the Cornerstone recognize?

What is the result for those who reject the Cornerstone?

Where does this leave those who have not trusted the Cornerstone?

Reread: 1 Peter 2:8

Also read:

Isaiah 8:14

1 Peter 4:17

1 Peter 1:14

1 Peter 1:22

What do you think it means when the Scripture speaks of people stumbling and falling? What happens to them?

For what reason do some people stumble and fall because of the Cornerstone?

Why do you think this stumbling has its root in not knowing and obeying God's Word? Please read the following verses and note what you see:

John 14:15

Luke 11:28

Psalm 119:105

John 14:21

Psalm 19:7-11

Hebrews 4:12

Psalm 119:9-11

Psalm 119 in its entirety (when you have time)

John 8:31-32

John 14:23

2 Timothy 3:16-17

John 13:34-35

2 John 1:6

James 1:22

1 Samuel 15:22-23

Joshua 1:8

James 1:22-24

John 5:24

1 John 5:3

Matthew 7:26

Ecclesiastes 12:13

If a person is disobedient, how might it cause someone else to stumble?

Have you seen this happen in the world today? Please explain.

Reread: 1 Peter 2:9

What four descriptors does Peter use in referring to those who have come to trust in Jesus? Please make a list.

1.

2.

3.

4.

What are the implications of believers being a chosen people, a royal priesthood, God's own possession and a holy nation?

From where are believers called?

To what are they headed and called?

How do you feel knowing that God has a very special purpose for your life?

Because of their position, in what way does Peter say God can and will use believers?

Note: It is of interest to see the description of those who have trusted in Jesus Christ, admittedly the Jewish Messiah. The same words used to describe them are also applied to the nation of Israel, especially in the Old Testament. While the roles and titles are somewhat similar, nowhere does it indicate that the "church" has replaced Israel in the plan of God. Furthermore, it is nowhere in Scripture indicated that the promises made to national Israel devolve upon the "church." Conversely, an honest and complete reading of the New and Old Testaments reveals that each group has distinct functions, duties, and destinies.

Reread: 1 Peter 2:10

How does Peter characterize a person's position both before and after trusting in Jesus Christ?

Before

   1.

   2.

After

    1.

    2.

Reread: 1 Peter 2:11

With what two labels did Peter characterize believers?

    1.

    2.

Note: The Greek word used for this concept as it applies to believers is *paroikous,* which literally means "those who live in a place that is not their home."

Read:

Hebrews 11:13

1 Peter 1:17

Why do you think Peter is again reminding his readers of their status in 1 Peter 2:11?

What warning does he give believers who have this status?

In what way do the things against which Peter warns his readers "wage war against one's soul?" Please explain.

When have you felt that you were at war with "sinful desires?"

Note: The Greek word used for "abstain" is *apechesthai* which literally means "to hold oneself constantly back from." Why is it hard for some people to abstain from sinful desires on their own?

Why do you think some people seem to be able to discipline themselves against negative action?

What impact does this have upon their lives?

Read:

James 4:1

Psalm 141:4

John 15:22

1 Peter 2:16

Romans 1:20

2 Corinthians 5:10

James 1:13-15

Do we have any real excuse if we choose to live contrary to the standards God sets before us?

What tools does God make available that enable believers to actually live the way He demands?

Read the following verses and note what you learn:

1 Corinthians 10:13

James 4:7

Galatians 5:16

Galatians 5:22-23

Ephesians 6:10-18

Hebrews 4:15

Psalm 119:11

Romans 12:2

1 John 2:1

Psalm 91:1-16

Matthew 4:1-11

James 4:8

Hebrews 2:1

Romans 13:13-14

1 Thessalonians 5:16-22

Psalm 1:1-2

Reread: 1 Peter 2:12

Also read: Colossians 4:5-6

In what way are believers to live among the citizens of this world? What four characteristics mentioned in these verses ought to be evident in our speech and conduct. Please make a list.

1.

2.

3.

4.

If believers evidence these characteristics in their daily lives, what two things will happen even if unbelievers accuse them of doing wrong?

1.

2.

Please think of an example when you have seen this in action.

Obviously, by including such concepts in His Word, God knows that we need directives, encouragement, strength and instruction to live as He intends. Why do we need this?

Please read the following verses for more insight on how we live and the impact it has on others, making notes along the way.

Matthew 5:16

Ephesians 2:10

Titus 3:5-8

James 2:18

1 Corinthians 6:20

1 Corinthians 6:19-20

What good deeds in your life do nonbelievers see?

How can we do good deeds so that they are both a witness and a discreet act of service (not merely for show)?

To what people can your good deeds be a witness?

Application Questions

From what specific sinful desires will you ask God to help you abstain this week?

What good deeds can you use as a witness to those around you?

How do you need to change your plans for the near future so that you will be an example to the unbelievers with whom you have regular contact?

Close in Prayer

IMPLEMENT GOD'S STANDARD
1 PETER 2:13-25

Open in Prayer

Group Warm-Up Questions

Who are some people who suffered for something in which they strongly believed?

How do people in different countries view and treat their leaders differently?

What is your general attitude toward people who are in authority over you?

Read 1 Peter 2:13-25

Reread: 1 Peter 2:13-14

Also read:

Romans 13:1-7

Titus 3:1-2

To whom did Peter urge his readers to submit?

Why is it often so difficult for us to submit to those who have authority over us?

What function does good and honest government serve?

Read:

John 18:1-11

Matthew 26:51-54

Acts 5:28-29

It would appear that perhaps Peter didn't always follow what seemed to be his overt advice. In the verses we just read we see him acting against:

    1. Religious leaders.

    2. Local politicians.

    3. Regional politicians.

    4. National rulers.

    5. An occupying military force.

    6. The equivalent of the local police.

How do his actions square with what we see in 1 Peter 2:13-14?

Read the following verses and note after each what God's Word says about how we ought to live, justice and the part of those who follow Him.

Matthew 17:24-27

Matthew 22:15-22

Ephesians 2:10

Romans 12:1

Romans 8:9

James 1:22

James 2:17

James 2:26

John 15:8

Acts 1:8

Romans 12:2

Luke 6:27-28

Deuteronomy 24:17

Deuteronomy 27:19

Matthew 25:40

James 1:27

Isaiah 1:17

Isaiah 56:1

Proverbs 21:15

Hosea 12:6

Psalm 106:3

Zechariah 7:9

Proverbs 21:3

Deuteronomy 16:20

Jeremiah 22:3

Amos 5:24

Reread: 1 Peter 2:15

What kind of lives should believers live?

How does it impact the enemies of believers if they live and act as God desires?

Reread: 1 Peter 2:16

Also read:

Galatians 5:1

Galatians 5:18

Galatians 5:13

Romans 6:22

In what ways are believers free?

In what way are believers God's slaves? (Remember, both Peter and Paul among others overtly refer to themselves as bond slaves in their letters.)

In what way are believers to not use their freedom?

Why do you think it is necessary for God to put forth this admonition in His Word?

Can you think of an example when someone has misused the freedom they had as a believer?

What was the result?

Reread: 1 Peter 2:17

Note: This particular verse encompasses several concepts that we can best understand if we dissect it in relationship to the original language. In effect, it provides us with four specific characteristics or commands endemic to the citizenship one enjoys when they have personally trusted Jesus Christ.

1. **Respect Everyone.**

   • The Greek word used here for respect is *timeisate*. In the most literal sense this translates to respect or honor in English. The implication is that believers are to be conscious of the fact that every human being has been created in God's image.

   • Interestingly we see the same word showing up in:

   Romans 12:10.

   Romans 13:7.

   1 Peter 3:7.

   Note: You may need to view these verses in several translations to get the full flavor of the meaning.

2. **Love the brotherhood of believers.**

- The word utilized for love in this instance is *agape*. *Agape* love refers to the self-sacrificial type of deep love that might cause a person to lay down their life to save another person. There is no higher word for love in the Greek New Testament.

3. **Fear God.**

- The Greek verb here is *phobeisthe*. This does not indicate sheer terror. Instead it indicates awe and reverence that leads to obedience. We see different forms of this same word in:

   1 Peter 1:17.

   1 Peter 3:16.

   2 Corinthians 7:11.

4. **Honor the king.**

- The Greek verb used at the beginning of this verse is *timaoi*. The honor or respect associated with this word is to be especially given to those God has placed in positions of authority such as we see in:

   1 Peter 2:13.

   1 Peter 2:14.

   Romans 13:1.

Who are believers to respect?

Does this include even those who are doing evil?

How can a believer show respect to someone who is not following God even while working to bring about positive change in opposition to that person?

Why do you think it is necessary for God to tell us to respect everyone?

What are the positive results when we act in this fashion? Please think of an example.

What are the negative results when we do not do this? Please give an example.

Who are believers told to love?

Why do you think God is again telling believers to love each other in this special fashion?

Read:

1 John 4:21

John 13:34-35

What impact does it have when believers follow this directive?

What impact does it have when believers do not follow this command?

Why is it necessary for the Holy Spirit to reinforce this concept to us a number of times through God's Word?

Reread: 1 Peter 2:18

Note 1: It is of interest that the Greek word used for slaves in this verse is *oiketai*, which was the common term for household or domestic servants. This is the same term used in:

Luke 16:13.

Romans 14:4.

Note 2: It is also of note that a high percentage of the early believers were in fact slaves. While there were certainly some considerate slave owners and masters, there were also many who were not and subjected their slaves to undeserved suffering and punishment. The Greek word used in 1 Peter 2:18 to describe these bad masters is *skolios*, which literally means "bent, curved, or not straight." The modern English medical term "scoliosis," which refers to a curvature of the spine, comes from this Greek origin.

To whom was this verse addressed?

Slavery was and is a detestable institution. It still exists in the world today in many forms. Please name those you can think of.

When have you suffered under someone's harsh authority?

Might this verse also apply to those who work for anyone who has authority over them? How so?

How are believers to act toward those who have authority over them?

In what circumstances are they to do this?

How does this relate back to the concepts we discussed around 1 Peter 2:13-14?

Read: Ephesians 6:5-9

In what ways does this relate to those engaged in an employer/employee relationship today?

Reread: 1 Peter 2:19

Why do you think God is pleased when believers endure unjust treatment?

Does this mean that one should not strive to improve their circumstances?

Think back again to our discussion around 1 Peter 2:13-14.

Also read 1 Corinthians 7:21.

Reread: 1 Peter 2:20

What is the difference between just and unjust suffering?

How does God regard each?

When have you suffered for doing good?

Reread: 1 Peter 2:21

Also read:

1 Peter 1:15

1 Peter 2:9

Note: The Greek word used in 1 Peter 2:21 for "example" is *hypogrammon*, which literally means "underwriting." This is not, however, the type of underwriting commonly thought of today. It refers to a writing or drawing produced by a student following the instruction of their teacher. Interestingly, it appears only once in the New Testament and that is in this one verse.

What does God call believers to do in regard to their conduct?

Who is to be our example?

Reread: 1 Peter 2:22-23

Also read:

Isaiah 53:9

2 Corinthians 5:21

Hebrews 4:15

1 John 3:5

Romans 12:19-20

How did Jesus Christ respond to insults and suffering?

What are the four specific things He did not do as cited in 1 Peter 2:22-23?

1.

2.

3.

4.

What is the one overriding thing Jesus did do?

How does this relate to us if we follow the admonition in 1 Peter 2:21?

What are some examples of when believers might follow this pattern in their lives?

Why is it hard to suffer in silence without retaliating?

What is the difference between retaliating and bringing about justice?

How does this relate to believers today? Please think of an example.

Reread: 1 Peter 2:24

Also read:

Isaiah 53:5

2 Corinthians 5:21

Romans 6:1-2

Romans 6:13

What did Christ do for us on the cross?

What did He accomplish by His actions and thus enable us to do and be?

What does it mean to you that "we are healed by His wounds?"

How, then, are believers to live?

Reread: 1 Peter 2:25

In what way are the believers to whom Peter was writing like sheep?

Does this also apply to people today? How so?

How did Peter's readers deal with this trait?

In what two ways is Jesus referred in this verse?

Note: The Greek word translated into these two descriptive terms is *episkopon*, which literally means "Shepherd" and "Overseer."

What do the terms used in the translation of the Bible you are using mean to you?

Read: Ezekiel 34:11-16

What further insight does this give you into the concepts of sheep and Shepherd in 1 Peter 2:25? Please make a list.

1.

2.

3.

4.

5.

6.

7.

Application Questions

To what authority (person or institution) should you submit and ask for God's help in doing so?

In what situation can you follow Christ's example of suffering without retaliating?

Close in Prayer

WIVES AND HUSBANDS
1 PETER 3:1-7

Open in Prayer

Group Warm-Up Questions

What examples would you point to in our society to illustrate our obsession with outward appearance?

What do you think is good and bad about the generally accepted cultural norms in society as they relate to the roles of men and women as they have changed over the last 20 years?

Read: 1 Peter 3:1-7

Keeping in mind that all Scripture works together and that understanding Biblical concepts requires looking at the whole of God's Word, please also read the following verses as a backdrop to Peter's discussion of wives and husbands:

Ephesians 5:21-33

Colossians 3:18-19

1 Corinthians 13

Reread: 1 Peter 3:1

What are some of the challenges of being a wife as observed by Peter?

Dr. Charles Missler said in reference to 1 Peter 3:1 "The command does not require women to be subordinate to men in general but to their husbands as a function of order within the home." What are your thoughts about what he said?

Reread: 1 Peter 3:1-2

Also read as a backdrop: Titus 2:3-5

Why did Peter encourage wives to "submit" to their husbands?

If a woman has a husband who is not a believer, what about her conduct and attitude might help him come to faith?

Reread: 1 Peter 3:3-4

Also read: 1 Timothy 2:9-11

What kinds of beauty can a woman have?

What kind of beauty is the most important?

How can the different types of beauty harm a woman's relationship with her husband if neglected?

Read: Colossians 4:5-6

How can the different types of beauty negatively or positively impact the representation of a relationship with God if a woman is a believer?

How can the different types of beauty work together for good?

Interesting note: The Greek word *cosmos* is the root of the English word "cosmetics" and means to bring order out of chaos.

Further note: Scripture in general does not forbid a measure of adornment of the person. However, it does make the point that depending upon this adornment to make one truly attractive as a person does not work. Conversely, a person who chooses to be slovenly, unwashed, disheveled, sloppy, and unhygienic generally repels others.

Reread: Colossians 4:5-6

While this reference relates to conduct, how might it also relate to the way a person grooms him or herself?

Might being tastefully attired and well groomed, whatever that means in one's station of life, enhance one's impact upon others?

Might a haughty spirit and bad tempter ruin one's impact despite good grooming and intellectual knowledge? Please explain.

Reread: 1 Peter 3:4-6

What is the advantage of a woman's inward beauty?

Reread: 1 Peter 3:3-6

What are the potential disadvantages of a woman's outer beauty?

What do you see as the potential advantages of a woman's positive outer appearance?

How can a woman evince outer beauty in a way that pleases God and enhances her representation as a follower of Jesus Christ?

1 Peter 3:5

What is the definition of real beauty in the eyes of God?

Putting all of the things we have so far discussed together, how can a godly woman make herself beautiful?

How is a man's or woman's impact upon others enhanced if they do their best to be well groomed within the limits of their ability?

How is a person's impact upon others diminished when they purposely neglect to care for what God has given them?

Why is it easier to be attractive on the outside rather than on the inside?

Larry Norman, generally acclaimed as the "Father of Christian Rock," penned the lyrics to a song entitled *Why Can't You be Good* to illustrate just such a situation. I present them here as an example of the potential dichotomy between outward and inward beauty.

Why can't you behave?

Why can't you be good?

You don't even try

To do the things you should

What is the reason?

I'd like to know,

Why you can't be good

You go into the bedroom

You say you gotta powder your nose

But the powder is cocaine

I see traces on your clothes

What is the reason?

I'd like to know

Why you can't be good

Take another look inside your dreams tonight

When you go to sleep

Try and find the reasons why you've lost your way

Like some little sheep

You say that you love me

That your heart is true

But you've got so many other loves,

What am I s'posed to do?

What is the reason?

I'd like to know

Why you can't be good

Take another look inside your dreams tonight

When you go to sleep

Try and find the reasons why you've lost your way

Like some little sheep

Your face looks so pretty

But your mind is such a mess

You got a cold and wicked heart that's beatin'

Underneath your breast

What is the reason?

I'd like to know

What is the reason?

I'd like to know

What is the reason?

I'd like to know

Why you can't be good

Why can't you be good?

Why can't you be good, baby?

You know you break my heart*

*Used by permission.

But wait.

As we have already alluded to, there is more at work in these verses than simple direction for women. Might some of these concepts apply to all believers regardless of gender?

Note: This is not intended to negate the definitive gender differences and roles of men and women.

Please reread 1 Peter 3:1-4 and list the things that might apply to men as well as women.

1.

2.

3.

4.

5.

Please read the following verses and discuss how the principles therein apply to all believers in a practical sense. I suggest you jot your thoughts down.

Colossians 3:23-24

Daniel 6:3-4

Titus 2:7-8

2 Corinthians 8:7

Proverbs 22:29

Ephesians 6:7-8

Joshua 1:8

Matthew 5:14-16

Ecclesiastes 9:10

Romans 12:2

1 Corinthians 10:31

Proverbs 3:5

Colossians 3:17

Proverbs 31:10

Philippians 1:9-10

Psalm 19:7-8

2 Timothy 2:15

Philippians 4:8

Deuteronomy 6:4-5

Reread: 1 Peter 3:7

What specific admonitions does Peter give to husbands? Please make a list.

    1.

    2.

    3.

What do you think it means that a husband should "honor" his wife?

What sort of a partner is a believing wife to a believing husband in experiencing God's gift of new life?

What is the impact upon a husband if he does not treat his wife properly?

How can a believer be sure to apply God's timeless standards for life instead of falling prey to changing cultural patterns of behavior?

If you are married, do you need to change the way you treat your spouse to be consistent with the timeless successful principles in God's Word?

Whether you are married or not, do you need to change the way you treat other people to be consistent with the timeless successful principles in God's Word? Please give an example if applicable.

Application Questions

What specific steps will you take this week to develop your inner character?

What can you do today to become a better spouse, friend, or fellow believer?

Close in Prayer

WEEK 6

SUFFERING FOR DOING GOOD
1 PETER 3:8-22

Open in Prayer

Group Warm-Up Questions

What childhood fight do you remember most vividly?

On a scale of one to ten, how good would you say you are at controlling your temper? (Assume that ten is very good and one is no control at all.)

Read: 1 Peter 3:8-22

Reread: 1 Peter 3:8

When is it hard for believers to live in harmony with each other? Why?

What specific directives did Peter give the believers to whom he was writing in this verse? Please make a list.

1.

2.

3.

4.

5.

Please go back over this list and discuss:

A. Why each positive characteristic of interaction between believers is so important.

B. What happens in a group of believers if they actually practice each individual characteristic?

C. What happens in a group of believers if they do not practice each specific admonition?

D. An example of when you have seen each particular thing in action or inaction?

How does it impact those who do not have a personal relationship with Jesus Christ when they see believers exhibiting these qualities as they relate to each other?

How does it impact non-believers when they do not see these characteristics of interaction evident from a group claiming to be believers?

Reread: 1 Peter 3:9

Here we see the list that began in the previous verse expanded, albeit in a slightly different fashion.

What specific things are believers told to not do? Again, please make a list.

1.

2.

Conversely, how are believers instructed to act when confronted with insults and evil action against them? Read the following verses as you construct your answer.

Romans 12:19

Leviticus 19:18

Proverbs 24:29

Proverbs 24:17-18

Matthew 5:44

1 Corinthians 4:12

How can believers still act to bring about justice, righteousness and truth in their relationships and world while adhering to these admonitions?

Note: This can be confusing to people without a holistic knowledge of the Scriptures. Followers of Jesus Christ are not called to be pacifists. They are called to be activists in bringing God's standards as clearly put forth in His Word to all facets of life and society.

Edmund Burke reportedly once said: "The only thing necessary for the triumph of evil is that good men should do nothing."

There is great danger in taking any portion of God's Word out of context. Indeed, many people have taken Matthew 5:39 out of context and used it as an excuse to let evil pervade in societies and organizations. Some would say that in the United States of America this misdirection resulted in:

1. The removal of Bible reading in public schools and a subsequent decline in behavior and performance.

2. The legalization of abortion and the subsequent removal of millions of tax paying citizens from the country leading ultimately to our financial ruin.

What are your thoughts about this?

Some have also observed that George Washington, the first president of the United States and often called the Father of the USA, was a follower of Jesus Christ. Had he not applied the whole truth of God's Word to life the United States might have remained a property of Great Britain, and slavery, which was institutionalized in England, might still exist in America on an official basis. What are your thoughts about these assertions?

We reviewed the following references in an earlier chapter on justice, life and the duties of believers and it would not hurt to revisit them.

Matthew 17:24-27

Matthew 22:15-22

Ephesians 2:10

Romans 12:1

Romans 8:9

James 1:22

James 2:17

James 2:26

John 15:8

Acts 1:8

Romans 12:2

Luke 6:27-28

Deuteronomy 24:17

Deuteronomy 27:19

Matthew 25:40

James 1:27

Isaiah 1:17

Isaiah 56:1

Proverbs 21:15

Hosea 12:6

Psalm 106:3

Zechariah 7:9-10

Proverbs 21:3

Deuteronomy 16:20

Jeremiah 22:3

Amos 5:24

How does it impact the enemies of believers if they live and act as God desires?

Suggestion: For further information on the correct application of God's Word to all of life I suggest you review "How to Avoid Error" in the appendices of this study guide.

Reread: 1 Peter 3:9

For what reason did Peter tell his readers to live at peace with everyone?

Reread: 1 Peter 3:10-12

Also read: Psalm 34:12-16

What must a person do who loves life and hopes for a long one? Please make a list.

    1.

    2.

    3.

    4.

    5.

    6.

Reread: 1 Peter 3:10

What two particular things does God tell us are important if we want to enjoy a life that is worth living?

Why do you think these two admonitions are so important?

Read the following verses to see what else we learn in God's Word about lies, liars and our speech.

Proverbs 13:5

Proverbs 12:22

Colossians 3:9

Exodus 23:1

1 Timothy 1:8-10

Revelation 21:8

Proverbs 6:16-19

1 Corinthians 6:9-11

James 1:26

1 Peter 3:10

Proverbs 30:5-6

Ephesians 4:15-16

Proverbs 12:19

Colossians 4:5-6

Ephesians 4:29-30

How does God regard liars?

Why do you think God speaks of liars as being on a par with murderers and those who are sexually immoral?

Conversely, what does God expect from the speech of a believer?

Reread: 1 Peter 3:11

Also read:

John 16:33

Matthew 5:9

What do you think it means to search for peace?

What is the difference between searching for peace and working to maintain it?

Reread: 1 Peter 3:12

Also read:

1 Thessalonians 5:22

Proverbs 1:20-33

How might you tie these verses together? Please explain.

Reread: 1 Peter 3:13

Also read:

Romans 8:28

Romans 8:31-39

How would you answer Peter's question?

Reread: 1 Peter 3:14

Also read: Isaiah 8:11-14

What happens when a believer suffers for doing what is right according to objective biblical standards?

How ought a believer to feel if threatened for doing right? Why?

Can you think of a time when you suffered for doing right? What happened?

Reread: 1 Peter 3:15-16

What else must a believer do when threatened for doing right?

If someone observes a believer's courage and attitude of trust in the Lord when threatened and asks about it, how should a believer respond?

Important Note: The use of the word "hope" in the Greek is the opposite of our use of the word in English. In the Greek, "hope" is a confidence, sureness, and knowledge of future things. In fact, in the Greek, the word "hope" infers a certainty stronger than knowing. It is an ultimate, internal, overpowering, all-enveloping eternal surety and truth that is absolute.

How should a believer explain the absolute assurance they have when questioned by a hostile or neutral witness?

What impact does a response of this nature have upon the questioner?

Read:

1 Peter 3:21

1 Peter 2:19

Acts 24:16

Romans 9:1

2 Corinthians 1:12

2 Corinthians 4:2-3

1 Timothy 1:5

1 Timothy 1:19

Hebrews 13:18

What is the best defense against slander?

If you are a believer, how prepared are you to explain the peace and confidence you have in Jesus Christ?

Again, assuming that you are a believer, what can you do to better prepare yourself for discussions about Jesus with friends who do not yet have a personal relationship with Him? Please make a list.

1.

2.

3.

4.

5.

6.

7.

Note: Here we see God's mandate for every believer to obtain proficiency in "defending the faith." This is termed the study of apologetics. Two excellent resources in the area are *Evidence That Demands a Verdict* by Josh McDowell and *In Defense of the Faith* by Dave Hunt. I suggest one of the group members provide a 10 minute report on *In Defense of the Faith* at a future meeting.

Reread: 1 Peter 3:17

When is it all right to suffer and when is it a waste?

Read: Hebrews 12:15

What can we do to be sure no "root of bitterness" rises up among a group of believers?

Why can this be so difficult for us as human beings when we feel that our hurt feelings are "justified?"

Reread: 1 Peter 3:18

About what specific things does Peter remind us regarding the death of Jesus?

Read: Romans 8:11

How, specifically, does this apply to us in the context of Peter's discussion?

Reread: 1 Peter 3:19-20

Through whom and to whom did Christ preach after His physical death?

What does this verse imply to anyone who says that God is unfair?

Reread: 1 Peter 3:20-21

What sort of prophetic picture do we see from what happened to Noah and his family in regard to the ark and the rest of society at the time? Please explain.

How, in reality, is it possible for people to be saved?

Read: Romans 6:3-5

How do Peter and Paul describe the function of baptism? (What do they say it is and is not?)

How has the death and resurrection of Jesus impacted your life?

Reread: 1 Peter 3:22

Where did Jesus go after His resurrection?

Also read:

Psalm 110:1

Hebrews 1:13

Hebrews 8:1-2

Hebrews 10:10-12

Hebrews 12:2

Colossians 1:15-16

Colossians 2:13-15

What else do these verses tell us about the power, position and function of Jesus' place at the right hand of God? Please make a list.

1.

2.

3.

4.

5.

6.

7.

8.

9.

10.

11.

12.

How does Jesus' place of authority at God's right hand make you feel about your relationship with Him?

Application Questions

What can you do over the next few days to promote harmony between you and the believers you know?

What response might you use when you are mistreated or insulted?

What steps can you take this week to become more prepared to answer questions about our hope and faith in Jesus Christ?

Close in Prayer

SUFFERING, ACCOUNTABILITY AND LOVE

1 PETER 4:1-11

Open in Prayer

Group Warm-Up Questions

In your opinion, what most distinguishes those who have legitimately trusted Yeshua Hamaschiach, the Jewish Messiah, who we refer to simply as Jesus in our culture, on a personal basis from those who have not?

If you knew for sure that the world would end in twenty-four hours and you were granted one wish for anything you want, for what would you wish?

Read: 1 Peter 4:1-11

Reread: 1 Peter 4:1

Why should believers expect to experience suffering?

What does it indicate if a person has suffered physically for their faith in Jesus Christ?

How might someone in your circumstances suffer for their faith? Please give an example.

Have you personally suffered because of your trust in Jesus? How so?

There is an old "Spiritual" song that goes:

I've come this far by faith

Leaning on the Lord

Trusting in His holy Word

He never failed me yet

In your mind, do the words of this song ring true despite suffering? How so?

What do you think it means to "be finished with sin"? (NLT)

Note: An examination of this phrase in the original language indicates that the believer has been freed from the dominance of sin and that it has no ruling power over one's life.

Read: Ephesians 6:10-18

In what other ways are believers to arm themselves? Please make a list.

1.

2.

3.

4.

5.

6.

7.

8.

9.

10.

11.

12.

13.

14.

Read: Romans 12:2

What further insight does this give you into preparing for conflict?

Reread: 1 Peter 4:2

What will believers not waste their time doing if they have suffered for their faith?

Conversely, what will they do?

Why do you think this truism exists?

What is the mechanism by which suffering leads to positive thought and action that is pleasing to God in the life of someone who has trusted Him and found new life through Jesus? Please explain how you see this working?

Is it possible that God sometimes uses suffering to prevent believers from participating in things that might dishonor Him? How so?

Reread: 1 Peter 4:3

What did some of those to whom Peter was writing do in the past?

Assuming that you have trusted Jesus, what are some of the pointless and wasteful things upon which you spent your time prior to that decision?

In the business world effective executives weigh the costs of engaging in certain activities. What might an objective executive see as the ultimate negative costs of the poor behaviors mentioned in this verse? Please make a list.

   1.

   2.

3.

4.

5.

6.

Reread: 1 Peter 4:4

Why are some of those with whom a believer engaged in wasteful practices prior to making a decision for God surprised when the life and focus of a believer changes?

How do one's former associates in wasteful living sometimes respond to the new and changed life of a believer?

Why do you think this is so?

What things about your lifestyle do unbelievers sometimes find unusual and seemingly unable to understand?

This verse indicates that unbelievers sometimes react violently when someone changes their behavior for the better and such unbelievers even slander friends who have made such a change. Why might they react with such vehemence and vituperation?

Does this seem strange to you, especially when the new life one is called to as a believer is, in the end, so much more profitable?

Read the following verses as you contemplate your answer:

John 14:6

John 10:10

John 16:33

In spite of this, with what human desires must believers still contend?

How are believers able to respond to these desires in a way that pleases God? Please read the following verses as you construct your answer.

1 Corinthians 10:13

Deuteronomy 31:6

Joshua 1:9

Isaiah 41:13

Matthew 10:28

1 Corinthians 16:13

Reread: 1 Peter 4:5

Also read: Matthew 12:36

In the end, who must face God and give an account of every thought, word and deed?

Does this include even those who choose to pretend to deny His existence or power?

Are you prepared for this last and final examination?

Reread: 1 Peter 4:6

Why is the Gospel presented to everyone, one way or another?

How do you think this relates to people in closed societies?

Reread: 1 Peter 4:7

What is coming soon?

What do you take this to mean?

Knowing this, how should believers respond? Please make a list.

1.

2.

3.

What do you think it means to be earnest in one's prayers?

Why was it necessary for God to remind us of this in His Word?

What happens when people are not earnest in their prayers?

What do you think it means to be disciplined in one's prayers?

Why was it necessary for God to remind us of this in His Word?

What happens when people are not disciplined in their prayers?

If you knew for certain that the world was going to end one year from now how would you think and act?

What specific things would you do during the course of the next twelve months if you knew that your life in this world would end in a year? Please make a list and imagine that your limit is seven specific actions.

1.

2.

3.

4.

5.

6.

7.

Reread: 1 Peter 4:8

Also read 1 Corinthians 13 for an amplification of this.

Why is it so important that believers show deep love for one another?

How do you see this working out in actual practice? What specific observable actions do you expect to see? Please make a list.

1.

2.

3.

4.

5.

6.

7.

What does it mean to you that "love covers a multitude of sins"? (NLT)

How do you see this working out in real life?

Read the following verses as you construct your answer.

Galatians 6:1

James 5:19-20

How does this operate in the face of the knowledge that everything we do or say has some sort of consequence? Please give some examples.

Why is it sometimes difficult to love other believers?

Reread: 1 Peter 4:9

What are believers encouraged to do?

To whom do you think we are to extend this hospitality?

How do you see this working out in actual practice?

Are there those to whom a believer should not extend this hospitality? Please explain and give an example.

Please read the following verses as you construct your answer:

Proverbs 13:5

Proverbs 29:27

1 Corinthians 15:33

1 Corinthians 5:11

Colossians 4:5-6

In the town in which I grew up a rough contractor named Lyle Brady and his wife became followers of Jesus and their lives changed. Shortly after their commitment several ex-convicts came through town claiming that they had accepted Jesus into their lives. Lyle and his wife essentially turned their home and vehicles over to them, simply handing them the keys, for a period of time.

What are your thoughts about this?

Reread: 1 Peter 4:10

Also read:

1 Corinthians 12:4-7

Galatians 5:22-23

Romans 12:4-8

1 Corinthians 12:8-11

Ephesians 4:10-12

Which believers in particular have received what we call "spiritual gifts?"

Please make a list of the gifts you believe God legitimately bestows upon believers based upon His Word:

1.

2.

3.

4.

5.

6.

7.

8.

9.

10.

11.

12.

13.

14.

15.

Are there other "gifts" or perhaps more rightly termed "talents" that a believer might have that are not specifically on this list?

How are those who have trusted Jesus to use the gifts they have received?

Reread 1 Peter 4:10 as well as Romans 12:3 as you think about this answer?

Reread: 1 Peter 4:11

Also read: Colossians 3:23-24

How are believers to conduct their lives as they exercise the gifts and abilities God has given them?

Is there any room for laziness or slackards in the application of God's gifts?

Why is there no room for mediocrity in the life of a person who has aligned themselves with the Ruler of the Universe?

What is the ultimate impact upon believers, unbelievers, and the world at large when the faithful exercise their gifts as instructed in the Word of God?

What is the impact when believers disobediently fail to wholeheartedly exercise their gifts and abilities?

How can we be sure to use what God has given us to the fullest?

Application Questions

In what simple way can you let unbelievers see that you live by a unique and objective set of priorities (emanating from the truth of God's Word) this week?

To whom will you offer hospitality this week and how will you do it?

Close in Prayer

FIERY TRIALS AND VICTORY
1 PETER 4:12-19

Open in Prayer

Group Warm-Up Questions

What is something for which you were wrongly punished when growing up?

When was the last time you were greatly surprised by something that happened to you?

Read: 1 Peter 4:12-19

Reread: 1 Peter 4:12

By what were Peter's readers to not be surprised?

What painful trials have you gone through during the time you have been a believer, if in fact you have made such a decision?

Note: The trials to which Peter was referring in the near term were far greater than many people today realize. He was referring to the pending destruction of the temple in Jerusalem and ravaging of the city exactly as foretold by Jesus Christ Himself. We can see this in:

Luke 19:43-44

Luke 21:20-24

Indeed, Jerusalem has been the subject of at least 118 conflicts over the centuries. Ardent students of the Scripture believe this first has to do with the place of Israel, including Jerusalem, in the plan of God. We see this in many places. Among them are:

Psalm 98:3

Psalm 121:4

Psalm 122:6

Zechariah 2:8-12

Second, in the case of the early believers, they were in the throes of two centuries of Roman persecution which would then be followed by 1,500 years of Papal persecutions.

Assignment: I suggest that one member of the group be assigned to read and provide a 10 minute report on *Our Hands are Stained with Blood* by Michael Brown for more information on such suffering.

Historical Aside: My friend, the Honorable Glenn Bates, is a Magisterial District Judge in Pennsylvania. Speaking of the rise and decline of nations and cultures he reminded me that:

1. There are observable and objective principles of behavior and conduct that lead to success for individuals, governments, cultures, and nations.

2. When these principles are violated the result in the end is failure and misery for all involved.

3. When these principles are adhered to they ultimately lead to justice and success.

4. Whether one realizes it or not these principles have their base in the Judeo-Christian Scriptures which we call the Bible.

5. When these principles are violated a negative downward pattern ensues including:

   - A decline in moral and spiritual values within the family.

   - As the family structure is weakened, members begin to neglect each other and act selfishly.

   - Material values tend to dominate decisions.

   - The roles of men and women become confused.

   - Marriage and divorce become more prevalent.

   - Absolutes and objective truth are ignored.

   - False ideas and subjective truth is given the same regard as eternal truth.

   - The decline in moral and spiritual values is exacerbated and extends from the family to the culture as well.

- Previous norms regarding sexuality become confused.

- People tend to place the highest value on material gain in the society and nation as a whole.

- The individual, nation, culture or civilization involved eventually disappears from the scene.

6. The negative downward spiral briefly described in point number 5 above can be reversed by adhering to the principles noted in point number 4.

7. This is corroborated in summary form by 2 Chronicles 7:14 which says:

   "Then if my people who are called by my name will humble themselves and pray and seek my face and turn from their wicked ways, I will hear from heaven and will forgive their sins and restore their land."

He also shared three quotes that he feels generally apply to most if not all societies.

George Santayana said that "those who forget the past are condemned to repeat it."

Hegel said "What experience and history teach us is this: that people and government never have learned anything from history or acted on principles deduced from it."

Winston Churchill also recognized these truths and is famously quoted as having done so.

Glenn points out that this has happened to many great civilizations including Greece, Persia, Babylon and Rome.

Read: James 1:25

What do you think believers should be doing in the light of Glenn's observations?

Reread: 1 Peter 4:13

Also read: John 15:18-21

What would participating in Jesus' suffering prepare the early believers for?

Does this also apply to those who follow and suffer for Jesus today? How so?

How can participating in Jesus' suffering prepare a person for His second coming? Please explain.

Reread: 1 Peter 4:14

Under what circumstances did Peter tell these believers they would be blessed?

According to this verse, how exactly does this happen? Who or what is the operant agent?

Can you think of a time when this in some fashion happened to you? What was the result?

Reread: 1 Peter 4:15

For what should believers not suffer? Please make a list.

1.

2.

3.

    4.

    5.

How is suffering for being a wrongdoer different from suffering for being a follower of Jesus Christ?

Reread: 1 Peter 4:16

Also read:

Matthew 5:10

2 Timothy 3:12

Acts 5:41

Have you ever been ashamed or hesitant to admit that you are a follower of Jesus Christ? Why?

How should believers respond if they suffer for their faith in Jesus Christ?

Note: In this verse we see believers referred to as "Christians." This is unusual in Scripture.

In Acts 11:24-26 we see that it was at Antioch believers were first called by this name. These verses specifically reference the efforts of one of the most well-known followers of Jesus who at this point was called "Saul." Saul, who later became known as "Paul," was a Jew like most early believers. We should also note that he was perhaps the most intelligent and highly educated man of his time. With most early believers being Jews, Christianity was most often considered a sect of Judaism.

In Acts 26:28 we find that even Agrippa had started to call the early believers by this name.

In what significant ways were Agrippa and others correct in considering Christianity a sect of Judaism? Please make a list.

1.

2.

3.

4.

5.

6.

7.

Note: It is a stain upon the history of the institutionalized church to see that for hundreds of years religious organizations took upon themselves the misnomer "Christian" as they persecuted both true Jewish and Gentile believers in a quest for power. We still see the results of this travesty today in both the secular and religious world. It has often been an obstacle to overcome for both Jews and Gentiles seeking a personal relationship with God. (This is detailed in *Our Hands are Stained with Blood* by Michael Brown.)

Please discuss how you have or have not seen this in actual practice.

Read:

Hebrews 12:7

1 Corinthians 10:13-14

Romans 5:3-5

James 1:2-5

Why might it be God's will for someone who loves Him to suffer?

What good can come out of suffering for someone who has trusted Jesus Christ? Please make a list.

1.

2.

3.

4.

5.

6.

7.

Read:

Romans 1:16

2 Timothy 1:12

Colossians 2:9

Colossians 1:15-17

For what reasons should believers not be ashamed of the Good News about Christ?

1.

2.

3.

4.

5.

6.

7.

In today's world people often say that they are spiritual and trust in something or someone. However, Scripture teaches that one's trust is only so good as the object in which it is placed. What does that mean to you in the context of today's discussion?

Reread: 1 Peter 4:17

What time did Peter say had come?

What do you think he meant by this?

About whom was he speaking when he spoke about those who had "obeyed the Good News?"

Conversely, about whom was he speaking when he referred to those who had "not obeyed the Good News?"

Note: The language employed in this verse infers that those who had not obeyed the Good News had an opportunity to do so and rejected it.

Reread: 1 Peter 4:18

In your own words, what does this tell us about the righteous and the ungodly?

Reread: 1 Peter 4:19

What do you think it means to suffer in a manner that pleases God?

What two things does Peter tell those who are suffering in a manner that pleases God to do?

    1.

    2.

What assurance does the Scripture provide for those who suffer in a manner that pleases God?

Note: Tertullian is known as the father of Latin Christianity. He was born the son of a Roman centurion in 145 AD and trained as a lawyer in Rome. In 185 AD he committed himself to the Jewish Messiah who we know as Jesus. He penned excellent works explaining the trinity and trained believers in the use of the Scriptures to refute heresies, in particular Gnosticism. He is to have said "custom without truth is only time-honored error." Most of his work was in defending Christianity against persecution from without or heresy within.

Speaking of Tertullian, Chuck Missler said "Tertullian declared that the blood of the martyrs is the seed of the church. Persecution can never destroy the Church of God. Its dangers lie within."

What do you think of what Dr. Missler said about Tertullian? Does it make sense to you? Please explain.

Application Questions

In what difficult circumstances to you need to praise, thank and rely upon God this week?

What steps do you need to take so that any suffering you are experiencing is not a result of your own wrongdoing?

Close in Prayer

LEADERSHIP, TEAMWORK, AND STRENGTH
1 PETER 5:1-14

Open in Prayer

Group Warm-Up Questions

What does the average person believe about the devil?

What people might consider you a leader or an example?

What motivates people to be leaders in various organizations?

Read: 1 Peter 5:1-14

Reread: 1 Peter 5:1

To whom did Peter first appeal in this passage?

In what three ways did Peter say he was like those to whom he addressed the first lines of this passage?

    1.

    2.

    3.

Why do you think Peter began this particular passage by speaking of his commonalities with those serving as elders?

Read:

Acts 11:30

Acts 20:17

Hebrews 13:17

Philippians 1:1

We see no hint of a professional group of people referred to as the "clergy" RULING over the other members of a fellowship in these verses.

What are your thoughts about this?

Read: Titus 1:7

What are some of the qualities God does not want in leaders?

    1.

    2.

    3.

4.

5.

6.

Read: 1 Timothy 3:1-7

Within these verses we find specific qualities that God:

1. Requires effective leaders in the body of believers to evidence in their lives.

2. Requires leaders in the body of believers to not have.

Let's take a look at these two important lists separately.

First, please list the qualities God requires of effective leaders as reflected in these verses.

(Please note that while this list is excellent and inspired it is not all inclusive and does not incorporate the totality of Scriptural guidance on the subject.)

1.

2.

3.

4.

5.

6.

7.

8.

   9.

   10.

   11.

   12.

   13.

   14.

Why do you think these specific qualities are so helpful to a person in a position of leadership?

Why do you think God demands and does not just suggest them?

Now please take a moment to list the qualities that God says should not be evident in the life of a person who is a leader in the body of believers.

   1.

   2.

   3.

   4.

   5.

Why do you think these specific qualities are so harmful to a person in a position of leadership?

Why do you think God demands and does not just suggest they be absent in the life of leaders?

Reread: 1 Peter 5:2-3

What specific things did Peter tell the elders to whom he was writing to do? Please enumerate.

1.

2.

3.

4.

Why, in your opinion, is it so effective when we do these things in our lives?

Note: We would do well to remember that Peter is passing on the instructions he received from Jesus Christ Himself to other believers in a position of leadership. To assist in this understanding let us recall some important portions of our study of the Book of John.

Read: John 21:15-22

Here we see Jesus asking Peter some important questions. Because of the limitations of language, especially English, many people gloss over this interchange thinking that Jesus kept asking the same question over and over. This is not entirely correct. As we will see, Jesus was asking three distinct questions for very specific reasons. In the end, while the questions are distinct, the result He was seeking was cohesive.

Before going further we should briefly look at the original language of the text. In Greek there are several types of love. This is delineated by the Greek words:

- *Eros*, which refers to the type of romantic or sexual attraction felt between two people. (*Eros* is the noun for this type of love. When expressed as a verb it appears as *eran*.)

- *Storge*, which refers to the love felt between family members as in a parent and a child. (*Storge* is the noun for this type of love. When used as a verb it appears as *stergein*.)

- *Philia*, which refers to "brotherly" love and is most often exhibited in a close friendship. (The noun for this type of love is *philia*, while the verb is *phileo*.)

- *Agape*, which refers to the self-sacrificial type of deep love that might cause a person to lay down their life to save another person. (*Agape* is the noun form of this love and *agapeo* is the verb form.) There is no higher word for love in the Greek New Testament.

The Bible speaks specifically of *philia* and *agape*. *Eros* and *storge* do not expressly appear in the Bible, although the concepts are obviously there.

Read: John 21:15

What question does Jesus ask Peter?

How does Peter answer?

Note: The Greek word Jesus uses for love in this verse is *agapeo*. The word Peter uses is *phileo*.

What significance do you attach to this fact?

What command does Jesus give to Peter as a result of the way Peter answered Jesus' question?

Note: An examination of the Greek is again helpful in figuring out what was going on here. The word Jesus used for feed was *boske* in which it is an active imperative and means to "keep on feeding." Furthermore, the word used for lambs is *arnos*, which refers to very little lambs (baby sheep).

What insight does this further understanding of the Greek give you?

Read: John 21:16

Note: The Greek word Jesus uses for love in this verse is again *agapeo*. Surprisingly the word Peter uses is still *phileo*.

What does Jesus ask Peter?

In what way does this question differ from the first time Jesus asked Peter if he loved Him? (Read the wording of each inquiry carefully.)

In your mind, what is the significance of this difference?

How does Peter answer Jesus?

What charge does Jesus give to Peter based upon Peter's answer?

How does the command Jesus gave in this instance differ from the one He gave after the first time He asked Peter if he loved Him?

Note: The Greek word used for "feeding in this instance is *poimaine* which indicates a shepherd continuously taking care of his flock. It comes from the same Greek word as pastor. The Greek word used for sheep in this instance is *probatia*, which refers to sheep that are more mature than the lambs referred to in Jesus' first charge to Peter.

What further insight might this understanding of the original language provide?

Read: John 21:17-19

Note: The Greek word Jesus uses for love in this verse is *phileo*. Peter also uses *phileo*.

What does Jesus ask Peter?

How does this differ from His first two questions to Peter?

Note: The word used for Peter's grief or pain is *lupeo*, which refers to the pain a woman might experience in a difficult childbirth that takes her to the point of death.

Why do you think this third question from Jesus grieved Peter so?

Further note: The Greek word used for feeding in this instance is the same as in the first charge. It is *boske* and involves continued feeding. However, the word used for sheep is somewhat different. It is *probata*, which refers to mature sheep.

Marching Orders

A summation of Jesus' marching orders to Peter would then appear to be:

1. Keep on feeding My little lambs.

2. Keep on shepherding My immature and growing sheep.

3. Keep on feeding My mature sheep.

As we can see from the book of John, Peter was at first a reluctant leader. This changed and he became a powerful "captain."

Reread: 1 Peter 5:2-3

What specific things does Peter tell the elders to whom he was addressing his comments to not do?

1.

2.

3.

Why do you think it is so harmful when people today do the things Peter told them to not do?

Note: While we earlier said that God's Word does not endorse a clerical order ruling over other believers in a draconian fashion, the problem did in fact turn up more than once and greatly displeased Jesus Christ. We see this quite clearly in Revelation 2:6.

In this verse we see a direct quote from Jesus Himself about the practices of the Nicolaitans.

What were these people doing that He found so abominable? To understand this verse we must first realize that the word "Nicolaitan" has its root in two Greek words:

1. The first word is Nicao, which means to conquer, overcome or rule.

2. The second word is Laos, which refers to the Laity (believers not part of the leadership) or people.

Putting this together we find that the term actually means to conquer the people. This group claimed apostolic authority and is believed to have been a sect that "lorded it over" the believers thus attempting to rob them of their freedom in Christ. History also records that this group was spiritually corrupt and actually engaged in idolatry and sexual sin. It was this group that brought into being the groups that we know today as clergy and laity. We see no such division in Scripture.

Read the following verses to see this and related problems clearly highlighted.

1. 3 John 9-11

    • Here we see problems arising from corrupt and arrogant leaders.

2. 1 Peter 2:9 and Revelation 1:6

    • Here we see that all believers are to serve as "kings and priests."

3. Hebrews 10:10

    • Here we find that all believers have equal access to God through Jesus Christ and they do not need a professional priest, minister, or pastor to mediate on their behalf.

What problems have arisen over the centuries from this practice of elevating certain people to positions of negative power or priesthood (virtual or literal) over other believers? Please list as many as you can think of.

1.

2.

3.

4.

5.

6.

Do you think Jesus feels the same way today about the deeds of certain individuals or groups as He felt about the Nicolaitans? How so?

Why does this bother our Lord so much?

What are the negative consequences of this type of problem?

We do, of course, see people with certain gifts placed in roles of leadership. However, these people, even with their admittedly important and crucial roles, are no better than those with other gifts. Dealing correctly with this concept has a direct impact upon the health of any small or large group of believers. Read the following verses to see what God has to say about gifts within the fellowship of believers:

Romans 12:4-12

1 Corinthians 12:4-31

1 Peter 4:10

Why do you think problems of this nature continue to crop up among people?

Note: In the words of Chuck Missler, leaders are to "feed and not fleece the flock."

What examples can you think of when this was done incorrectly? What was the result?

When have you seen this done correctly? What was the result?

Reread: 1 Peter 5:4

What did Peter tell the leaders among the early believers to expect if they acted in accordance with God's pattern for leadership?

If you are part of a group or groups of believers, what leadership styles have you observed?

Which leadership patterns do you feel are most effective? Why?

Reread: 1 Peter 5:5

To whom does Peter begin to turn his comments in this verse?

What common thing does he say should characterize the interaction between those who are mature and those who are younger?

Christianbiblereference.org speaks of humility in this manner:

"In the Bible, humility or humbleness is a quality of being courteously respectful of others. It is the opposite of aggressiveness, arrogance, boastfulness and vanity."

Why do you think it is so important that good leaders exhibit humility? What positive things come of it?

Why do you think it is important that those not yet more experienced also display humility? What are the positive results?

What happens when more experienced and less experienced people in a group do not show humility toward each other when they interact?

What do you think this verse means when it says "God opposes the proud but gives grace to the humble"?

Is there both a positive and negative fashion in which pride might be manifested? Please read the following verses as you think about your answer.

Romans 12:3

Romans 12:16

Philippians 2:3

Genesis 3:19

Colossians 3:23-24

Ephesians 6:5-9

It would appear that pride can be exhibited in both a positive and negative fashion. Merriam Webster defines the negative type of pride succinctly as inordinate self-esteem or conceit.

Conversely, this same dictionary describes the more positive side of pride as a reasonable or justifiable self-respect.

Vocabulary.com says "*Pride* as a noun describes a feeling of happiness that comes from achieving something. When you do a good job or finish a difficult task, you feel *pride*.

Pride also acts as a verb meaning "be proud of." You might *pride* yourself on being punctual, or *pride* yourself on always having a daring, trendsetting haircut.

How would you sum up the concepts of both proper and improper pride and humility?

What happens when people adhere to the biblical principles of proper and positive pride and humility?

Reread: 1 Peter 5:6

Note: Going forward from this point Peter seems to be addressing both the elders as well as those who are younger.

What is the first thing he admonishes all believers to do?

What does he say will be the result of this?

Why is it sometimes difficult to be submissive to those in authority over us?

How can we do this and still be true to God's Word?

Read:

John 21:22

Acts 4:18-19

What should we do in our personal lives if those who are in leadership positions are clearly not following the admonitions of Scripture?

Reread: 1 Peter 5:7

Also read:

Matthew 6:25-32

Psalm 55:22

What does God want us to do with our worries?

How can we do this operationally on a daily basis?

Hint: We are not the first people to face this dilemma. 1 Thessalonians 5:16-22 provides some helpful principles. Please list them.

    1.

    2.

    3.

    4.

    5.

6.

7.

Why do these principles, when followed in one's life, work so well?

How does it make you feel to know that God cares about even the smallest details of your life?

Reread: 1 Peter 5:8

Who is the great enemy of believers?

What is this great enemy always doing?

Why is he a greater enemy to believers than to non-believers?

What do you think it means that he is looking to "devour" those who have trusted Jesus Christ?

Why is his influence upon non-believers so bad for them whether or not they know about it?

Why should believers not discount the power of our adversary?

These verses warn believers to stay alert as they watch out for their adversary. Why is this state of vigilance so necessary?

What are some of the subtle stratagems employed by Satan?

Read:

2 Timothy 3:16-17

Hebrews 4:12

Ephesians 6:17

What particular weapon must we utilize in this cosmic battle between good and evil?

Read:

Deuteronomy 20:4

Isaiah 8:11-14

1 Thessalonians 5:16-22 (for the second time in this session)

How should we think and what should we know and do on a daily basis as we engage in this battle?

Why do you think these same principles are so effective in not only combatting worry, but in actually combatting our adversary?

Reread: 1 Peter 5:9

Also read:

Ephesians 6:10-18

Ephesians 1:19-22

Colossians 2:8-10

Romans 10:13

2 Timothy 1:7

Acts 4:11-12

Colossians 2:13-17

How should we face our great adversary?

How does this relate to fellow believers around the world?

Why are believers who are endeavoring to do the will of God while influencing those around them with His Word and principles particularly "under attack"?

Read:

Revelation 3:15-16

Revelation 3:17

Matthew 10:37

John 12:25

Why are those who say they are believers but do not make any effort to influence their world for Jesus Christ not seem to be of any consequence to our enemy? Why does he seem to not be bothered by them?

Are those who say they are believers but do not engage in the daily cosmic battle actually doing more harm than good? How so?

Read:

Acts 20:24

Revelation 12:11

Revelation 17:14

By what power do we defeat him and his minions?

How can you be an example to those around you?

Reread: 1 Peter 5:10

Also read:

2 Corinthians 4:7

2 Corinthians 4:17

To what did Peter say believers are called?

What do you think he meant by this?

What did Peter say God would do for these believers after they suffered for a while? Please list these actions in order.

1.

2.

3.

4.

Do you think that the items on this list are in the order presented on purpose?

If so, why do you think that might be?

When have you suffered as a believer and what was the result?

Read: Romans 5:3-5

What other insights do these verses give you into the suffering Peter writes about in his first letter? There are at least seven for us to glean. Please list them.

1.

2.

3.

4.

5.

6.

7.

Reread: 1 Peter 5:11

For what purpose do you think we are reminded of this directly after a discussion about suffering?

How does this simple statement impact you?

Reread: 1 Peter 5:12

Who helped Peter write this letter?

Note: The older translations of this letter name the person who helped Peter with this letter as Silvanus. An amanuensis is a person who essentially writes down what someone else dictates to them. The person doing the dictating is the author of what is produced, but he or she could not have done it without the help of their amanuensis. It is thought that Silvanus may have personally delivered the letter which we know as 1 Peter to the churches in Pontus, Galatia, Cappadocia, Asia and Bithynia.

More recent translations, making the assumption that Silvanus is the same person as the Silas who accompanied Paul on his second missionary journey, simply inserted the name Silas in the text. This is certainly plausible, although the names were common at that time.

What did Peter tell his readers about Silas?

What three things did Peter hope to accomplish with his letter? Please make a list.

   1.

   2.

   3.

How do you understand God's grace to enter into this equation?

Note: Grace has been defined as getting what we don't deserve.

Conversely, mercy has been defined as not getting what we do deserve.

How do you see these two concepts working together?

Reread: 1 Peter 5:13

Who else sent their greetings along with Peter's letter?

Note: The "church at Babylon" has sometimes been assumed to have been a code word for the pagan culture of Rome. However, the Nestorian church was held from the beginning at the ancient city of Babylon on the Euphrates River. The Coptic Church has long claimed that this refers to a settlement known as a new Babylon located near present day Cairo. While we will someday know the answer to this question for certain, our questions about this in no way detract from the power, inerrancy and infallibility of this letter as part of the Canon of Scripture.

Note 2: The Marcus or Mark referred served as Peter's amanuensis for the Gospel of Mark. The inclusion in some translations of the Jewish rendition of Mark (Marcus) simply helps us to realize the Jewishness of the New and Old Testaments as they flow together into one cohesive document. This is the same Marcus who earlier had not yet been up to the job of working with the disciples but later matured into a faithful and valued team member.

See: Acts 15:37-39

2 Timothy 4:11

What hope does Marcus' growth into such a vital part of God's work give to new believers today?

Reread: 1 Peter 5:14

How did Peter tell the believers to whom he was writing to greet each other?

Note: This was a common and appropriate form of enthusiastic greeting between good friends two thousand years ago in the culture in which Peter lived.

What kind of greeting do you think is both appropriate and enthusiastic in the culture in which you find yourself? Please explain.

What wish did he extend to the believers who were to read his letter?

Does this extend to us today?

Application Questions

What changes might you make in the way you lead in order to be more effective?

What worries will you turn over to God today?

In what area of life will you ask God to help you be properly humble this week?

Close in Prayer

INTRODUCTION TO THE SECOND LETTER OF PETER

Peter's second letter was written shortly after his first. Archaeologists and theologians date it to between 65 and 68 A.D., approximately 30 years after the murder and resurrection of Jesus Christ.

Interestingly, it appears to have been written shortly after the death of the apostle Paul. This knowledge helps us to better understand the references Peter makes to Paul's letters in this, his second letter. We might note that Peter specifically references all of Paul's letters being already in circulation.

It is also interesting to note that in the first few centuries after it was written some people disputed the letter and its authenticity. Even though it was well accepted through most of the world by the fourth century there were still those who doubted it. This was most likely because they did not want to hear what it said as it might apply to them. In his typically straight forward manner Peter discusses Scripture, prophecy, and false teachers. As one might expect of a letter inspired by the Holy Spirit and written by Peter, he pulls no punches when dealing with false teachers. He hits them hard.

As in all cases involving Scripture, archaeological finds have further authenticated his second letter beyond any doubt. Portions of it were found in Cave 7 at the ancient Qumran site in Israel. This was detailed by Jose O'Callaghan in his "Los papiros griegos de la cuerva 7 de Qumran," Madrid, *Biblioteca de Sutores Cristianos*, 1974, pp. 74-75, plate v. These fragments were found along with the Gospel of Mark and this second letter is now thought to have been a covering document to the Gospel itself. It is of note that this cave was sealed in 68 A.D. shortly before the Jewish War to preserve the contents from destruction by the enemies of Israel.

This letter was Peter's final message just prior to his being murdered by the Roman authorities. It stands out for its prophecies, hard-hitting exhortations, and warnings about the apostasies to come. This is, of course, what has made many teachers uncomfortable and at the same time has made the letter so powerful, helpful and influential.

WEEK 10

CALL TO EXCELLENCE
2 PETER 1:1-11

Open in Prayer

Group Warm-Up Questions

What qualities of character do you find most attractive in other people?

If you could be better at one thing, what would you want to improve?

Read: 2 Peter 1:1-11

Reread: 2 Peter 1:1

How does Peter describe himself in the opening sentence of this letter? What two things does he mention?

Why do you think these two descriptors seem to mean so much to him and to summarize his life?

To whom is Peter writing?

Where did those to whom Peter is writing obtain what they have in common with Peter?

What qualities of Jesus Christ made this possible? Please explain how you see this working.

Does this letter then take on a timeless quality as we read it today? How so.

Reread: 2 Peter 1:2

What three specific things does Peter pray God will give his readers? Please list them.

    1.

    2.

    3.

Why were these three things so important to the early believers?

Why are these three things so important in the world today?

What do you see as the relationship between knowledge of God and spiritual growth?

Reread: 2 Peter 1:3

What, in short, has God given believers?

How is He able to do this?

How are we able to receive what He has made available to all believers? What did we do?

By what means did and does God call believers to Himself?

What do you think it means that He makes this call by means of His glory and excellence?

How does His glory and excellence call people to Him in practical terms? Please think of an example.

How equipped do you feel for life and godliness?

Why are the objective qualities we find in God's Word necessary for the godliness He desires in contrast to the godliness claimed by those not yet believers?

Note: Peter often spoke of power. The Greek word used in his letters was *dunamis* and we see it in:

1 Peter 1:5

1 Peter 3:22

2 Peter 1:3

2 Peter 1:16

2 Peter 2:11

We know there are no coincidences in Scripture. Every word, every place name, every form of punctuation is there by design. Why, then, does Peter so often speak of power?

We know Peter was a very physically powerful individual seemingly without fear. Witness:

1. John 21:6 and John 21:11 when Peter singlehandedly pulled a very heavy net to shore that 7 other disciples working together were unable to draw in. (The 153 fish recorded in this net likely each weighed between 5 and 10 pounds for a total weight between 765 and 1530 pounds with the further hindrance of the water involved.)

2. John 18:10 when over 600 battle hardened soldiers came to arrest Jesus, and Peter thought the best course of action was to singlehandedly attack them (which he did with great enthusiasm).

Could it be that the Power of Jesus Christ particularly impacted him since he was, in human terms, so physically powerful? What do you think?

Are you as a person especially impacted by certain qualities or actions of Jesus because of your background? How so?

Reread: 2 Peter 1:4

What has God given people because of His glory and excellence?

With what two words are these promises described?

    1.

    2.

What specific things does Peter say these promises enable people to do?

    1.

    2.

What human condition makes it necessary for us to appropriate the power inherent in what these promises can do for us when accepted?

An expansion of the concepts in this verse can be seen by combining what we see here with other applicable verses. See:

1 Peter 1:3

1 Peter 1:5

2 Peter 1:3

Romans 8:9

Galatians 2:20

What are your thoughts about this progression?

How do you see all of this working together?

Reread: 2 Peter 1:5

What specific effort does Peter tell his readers to do in regard to God's promises?

Why does God desire a response from us when He gives us these precious promises?

If we do not respond to God's promises, of what is this evidence?

Looking back to the verses preceding 2 Peter 1:5, to what is Peter referring when he says "In view of this"? (NLT) Please make a list.

1.

2.

3.

4.

5.

6.

7.

Reread: 2 Peter 1:5-7

What specific things do we find in these verses that believers are to do in response to the promises of God? Please list them.

1.

2.

3.

4.

5.

6.

7.

8.

Note: In the Tanakh, what the Jews call the Old Testament, God provided Ten Commandments. They were not ten suggestions.

Do you think the list we just made detailing what God says believers are to do in response to His promises are suggestions or directives? How so?

Which of the qualities listed in 2 Peter 1:5-7 do you find most difficult to exhibit?

Which of the qualities just listed do you most want to see undeniably evident in your life?

In order to add to our understanding of these few verses let's take a look at the original Greek. Here we find that the word used for "add" is in the imperative and comes from the Greek word *epichoregesate*.

- This is our first clue as we realize that this action is essentially in the form of something God commands us to do. It is not a suggestion.

- Our second clue comes as we realize that *epichoregesate* is the root of the English words "chorus," "choreograph," and "choreography." It indicates that these qualities are intended to be acting together and simultaneously in the life of a follower of Jesus Christ. They are not only complimentary, but the final whole or "chorus" produced in one's life is like a beautiful song to God. (Read Psalm 96:1-3 and 2 Corinthians 2:15 and discuss how they might relate to this concept.)

- The third clue comes from the original language and the practices in place at the time Peter was writing. In ancient Greece the choir director paid the training expenses for the chorus. In a similar fashion the Messiah has paid our way so that we can see these qualities develop in us so that we can live a worthwhile life. (Read 1 Timothy 2:6 and John 10:10 to see this playing out in Scripture.)

- The fourth clue comes when we realize that the "virtue" or "moral excellence" spoken of in these verses is actually akin to the valor exhibited by a good and courageous soldier. All followers of Jesus Christ are actually participant soldiers. Larry Norman, "the Father of Christian Rock," was getting at this when he encouraged his fans to be part of the "Solid Rock Army."

Reread: 2 Peter 1:8

What does God promise will happen to us if we grow as He directs in the previous three verses?

Reread: 2 Peter 1:9

Note: The Greek words used in this verse that are translated blind are *typhlos* and *myopazon* (from which we derive the English word "myopic.") Taken together they mean "unable to discern spiritual things."

What do we learn about those who refuse or fail to grow as God intends as detailed in 1 Peter 1:5-7?

Do you think failure to grow as God intends is a matter of purposeful neglect or irresponsible failure? How so?

How is it possible that people forget what God has done for them? How does this sometimes happen?

Reread: 2 Peter 1:10

What are believers to do in order to be sure they are developing as God intends and as Peter has detailed in verses 5-7 of this chapter?

What promise do we have if we follow these directives from God's inerrant Word?

Note: The Greek word utilized for stumble in this verse is *ptaiseite*. This does not infer that a believer loses their salvation, or that salvation depends upon spiritual growth. *Ptaiseite* means to trip up or to experience a reversal. However, as stated in 1 Peter 1:10 a believer who is growing and maturing in accordance with God's desire for us and the tools He has provided can claim His promise. It is when one errs and goes their own way that they run into problems.

This, of course, raises a question in minds of some people. That is, if the Creator of the Universe, with all knowledge and power, has given us a formula for lifetime success in His written Word, why would anyone think they can improve upon it by going their own way? What do you think?

Reread: 2 Peter 1:11

What is also promised to those who adhere to God's Word and grow toward maturation and consistent victory according to His will?

What do you take this to mean?

Note: After reviewing some of today's verses in a Bible study, one of the participants, Ed Vandegrift, mentioned an interesting exercise from his personal study. He suggested that it might be beneficial to explain the differences between the following concepts in one's own words. The concepts and short definitions he cited were:

1. Transformation: A change of character from within.

2. Conformation: Agreeing with and/or following rules of conduct.

3. Reformation: Improvement in conduct.

He suggested that while conformation and reformation are the result of transformation, they might also be part of a process leading up to it. What do you think?

Application Questions

What godly and Scriptural quality might you add to your faith at this point in time?

What steps will you take this week to make your faith more effective and productive?

What can you do to "be sure" of your place as a person God has called?

Close in Prayer

WEEK 11

THE POWER OF PROPHECY
2 PETER 1:12-21

Open in Prayer

Group Warm-Up Questions

If you knew you were about to die and had time to make only one phone call or write one letter, whom would you contact? Why?

To what interesting event have you been an eyewitness?

Read: 2 Peter 1:12-21

Reread: 2 Peter 1:12

In what did Peter say his readers were already established?

What did he mean by this?

Why is it that we as human beings seem to need constant reminders about such things even though we already know them?

How might a daily time spent reading God's Word and in prayer help to make this a reality in the life of a believer?

If you knew that your favorite author who you once had met was coming to town soon and you were going to have the chance to have dinner with him or her, how would you prepare?

Would you reread what they have written so as to make intelligent conversation?

Would you learn all you can about them?

If possible, might you call them prior to their visit to further prepare you for the evening?

How might you apply this to the imminent return of Jesus Christ?

Reread: 2 Peter 1:13

What did Peter say it was only right to do?

For how long did Peter say he should do this?

Read: John 21:15-19

How do you see these verses tying in with 2 Peter 1:13?

Was Peter, when writing his second letter, simply doing what he thought was right or following a long-standing command directly from Jesus Christ?

How do you see these directives from Jesus Christ Himself as they relate to some or all of His followers today? Please explain.

Reread: 2 Peter 1:14

What did Peter know would soon happen?

Reread: 2 Peter 1:15

What did Peter want his readers to be able to do after he was gone?

Why do you think he was working so hard to do this?

As we saw in John 21:15-19 Peter, a formerly strong man, was given some insight into his future death by Jesus. He was, in fact, crucified upside down when it came to that point as he felt he was not worthy to be crucified upright in the same manner as his Lord.

Read the following verses and jot down how you see them applying to both Peter's life and death as well as yours.

John 21:18-19

Philippians 1:23

2 Corinthians 5:1-10

1 Peter 1:1

1 Peter 1:17

1 Peter 2:11

How many years do you think you have before you die?

How many weekends do you think you might have left?

How many Christmases do you think you have still coming?

How many more New Years do you expect to celebrate?

With the answers to these questions in mind, how should the verses we just read impact your daily life? Please explain.

Reread: 2 Peter 1:16

What did Peter say that he and the others were not doing?

What had they seen with their own eyes?

Note: As Chuck Missler stated, "true faith is founded on historical facts, which eyewitnesses corroborated." Any sincere and diligent student of history realizes that the documents which we call "The Bible" are the most authenticated and accurate known to man. Any statement to the contrary is most markedly made by a person who cannot accurately claim to any reasonable level of scholarship in the fields of history, archaeology and epistemology.

We might also note that the doctrine of the second coming of Jesus Christ was a key part of not only the New and Old Testament documents, but also in particular of Peter's preaching. We can see Peter's emphasis on this clearly in:

1 Peter 1:5

1 Peter 1:13

1 Peter 4:13

2 Peter 1:16

Acts 2:32-33

Acts 2:36

Acts 3:16

Acts 3:20-21

Reread: 2 Peter 1:17

What had he and the others heard audibly and directly from the majestic glory of God?

What did God say about Jesus?

Reread: 2 Peter 1:18

Where were they when they heard this audible proclamation from God?

Reread: 2 Peter 1:19

What did the experience on the holy mountain do for those who heard it?

Why do you think this gave them even greater confidence in the message proclaimed by the prophets?

What did Peter admonish his readers to do in relationship to what the prophets wrote?

Note: At the time Jesus walked the earth the Tanakh, what Jews call the Old Testament, was the only Scripture in existence.

To what did Peter liken the writings of the Old Testament prophets?

For how long did he expect their words to act like a shining lamp?

How do you see this operating in actual practice?

Note: For some additional insight into this please take the time to review *Composite Probability and the Judeo-Christian Scriptures* in the appendices of this material. One might also benefit from the briefing package entitled *The Footprints of the Messiah* from Koinonia House Publishing.

Reread: 2 Peter 1:20-21

Where does Peter tell us real prophecy does not come from?

    1.

    2.

How does Peter tell us real prophecy does come about?

    1.

    2.

Peter uses the Greek word *pheromenoi* when describing how the men who recorded Scripture were inspired. This word literally means to be "borne along" or "carried along." In various versions of the Bible we most often see it translated into English as "moved." This same word also appears in Acts 27:15 and Acts 27:17 where it is said that sailors aboard a ship "let it run before the gale (powerful wind) and that they "were driven before the wind."

How does this greater understanding of the original language help us further understand how the New and Old Testaments came into being? Please explain.

Note: For further information on Scripture as well as its accurate interpretation and application to all of life please see *How to Avoid Error* in the appendices of this book. Every serious believer and student of the Scriptures should master these principles.

Application Questions

If you do not have a daily prescheduled time to read the Bible and pray, how might you fit it into your life from this point on?

What portion of Scripture that you have neglected lately will you take the time to study this week?

How can you read the Bible differently this week in light of its importance?

Close in Prayer

WEEK 12

FALSE TEACHERS
2 PETER 2:1-22

Open in Prayer

Group Warm-Up Questions

What is your favorite proverb or wise saying (for example, "All work and no play makes Jack a dull boy")?

In what ways do people today abuse their freedom?

Read: 2 Peter 2:1-22

Note: False teachers have plagued faithful followers of the God of the Bible and His Jewish Messiah since Satan rebelled against Him. Examples of this can be seen throughout the Old Testament as well as in the New. We can see this in many places including:

Deuteronomy 13:1-3

Deuteronomy 18:20-22

Ezekiel 13:9

Jeremiah 5:30-31

Jeremiah 14:14-16

Jeremiah 23:16

Jeremiah 23:21

Lamentations 2:14

Luke 6:26

Matthew 24:24

2 Timothy 4:3-4

Acts 20:28-30

2 Peter 3:14-18

1 John 4:1-6

Mathew 7:15-16

2 Corinthians 11:1-4

2 Corinthians 11:13-15

1 Timothy 6:3-5

Jude 1:4

Colossians 2:8

Galatians 1:6-9

Romans 16:17-18

2 Timothy 3:13

Matthew 24:11

1 Timothy 6:20-21

Acts 20:29

1 Timothy 4:1-3

Matthew 24:4-5

Revelation 22:18-19

2 John 1:1-7

Ephesians 5:6

Mark 13:22

2 John 1:7-11

Revelation 21:8

Ezekiel 13:3

Jeremiah 23:9-18

Note: Furthermore, we should remember the all-pervasive negative impact of false teachers as explained by the Apostle Paul. Speaking about false teaching, this highly intelligent, educated and erudite scholar said:

"This false teaching is like a little yeast that spreads through the whole batch of dough!" (Galatians 5:9) (NLT)

Reread: 2 Peter 2:1

Note 1: In this verse Peter speaks about destructive heresies. This should lead us to ask what constitutes a heresy. For the purposes of an honest and believing student of the Judeo-Christian Scriptures, we can succinctly describe a heresy as any belief or teaching that is counter to the clear teaching of the Bible, which we know as the Word of God. For the purposes of brevity, efficiency and effectiveness I point to two resources that will help one to avoid such errors. They are:

1. *Exegetical Fallacies* by D. A. Carson published in 1996 by Baker Academic, a division of Baker Publishing Group in Grand Rapids, Michigan.

2. "How to Avoid Error" in the appendices of this book and all of the books in the Dynamic Bible Studies series.

Note 2: Peter points out two overriding themes that characterize the cancer fomented by false teachers. Everything else they do is focused on accomplishing these two goals.

What two all-influencing things did Peter warn his readers that false prophets would do?

1.

2.

How does it help us to realize that these are the ultimate goals of false teachers?

Why, in particular, do you think these are the overriding goals of false teachers?

Based upon this verse, what impact does it have upon false teachers themselves when they participate in this program of destructive negative propaganda?

Why do false teachers seem to persist even when they realize the destructive impact of what they are doing and teaching upon themselves?

Reread: 2 Peter 2:2

How successful did Peter say false teachers would be?

Is it uncommon for people to follow false teachers today?

Why do you think this is so?

In 2 Peter 2:2 we see two activities that characterize the practices of false teachers. What are they?

    1.

    2.

What is the net result of the efforts of false teachers?

How do you see this relating back to 2 Peter 2:1?

Reread: 2 Peter 2:3

What common practice does Peter warn that we will see from false teachers?

What seems to be the result of this practice?

Why do you think they do this?

What does Peter tell us will be the ultimate result of this practice?

When was the penalty for their abhorrent behavior decided upon?

Note: Sometimes believers would like to see this result come to pass sooner rather than later. At times it seems to occur and at others it takes longer than we might prefer. Why do you think God does this in His own time? See 2 Peter 3:9 as you construct your answer.

Reread: 2 Peter 2:4

What did God do to the angels who had sinned?

Reread: 2 Peter 2:5

In what way did God deal with the disobedient ancient world?

Whom did God protect in the ancient world? Why?

Note: Before going on we should realize that Genesis, wherein we see the Flood of Noah recorded, is actual history. Besides being revealed in God's Word we also find this corroborated by good scholarship. In that regard one might find it helpful to review the series *Is Genesis History?* by Del Tackett as well as the myriad scientific work of Creation Ministries International and similar organizations.

Why do believers find it helpful to know that what we find in the Bible is attested to by good scholarship?

Why and how can this be particularly helpful to non-believers who are considering the claims of Scripture?

Reread: 2 Peter 2:6

Also read: Jude 7

What happened to the cities of Sodom and Gomorrah?

For what purpose did He do this?

Note: The name of the city of Sodom is the root of the English word sodomy, which refers to a deviant sexual practice among males engaged in same sex relationships. Some people in today's world might suggest this is "normal," but God disagrees and tells us it is self-destructive (See Romans 1:26-27). As pointed out in a recent class and corroborated by a class member in the field of psychology, people engaged in same sex relationships suffer a higher rate of ill health, disease, early death, mental problems and suicide.

God's Word is replete with information on the solution to the difficulties suffered by people experiencing these and other similar situations. We might find it helpful to keep the principles found in the following verses in mind as we consider a few questions.

Please read:

John 14:6

John 15:4

Ephesians 3:16-19

1 John 2:27

2 Corinthians 5:17

What solution do the people suffering from the problems referenced in 2 Peter 2:6 and Jude 7 need?

What solution do people suffering from other sorts of problems or sinful behavior need?

Reread: 2 Peter 2:7-8

Who was Lot?

What kind of a man was he?

How did living in Sodom impact him?

Did he allow himself to be influenced by the negative culture in which he was living? How so?

What did God do for Lot?

Reread: 2 Peter 2:9

How does God deal with those who are ungodly as well as those who are righteous?

In today's world one sometimes hears unbelievers claiming that people they see who are following Jesus are "ungodly."

Why do you think they might say such a thing?

By what arbitrary standards are those making such statements generally judging?

In what way is it ironic and even hypocritical for those making such statements to engage in the type of "judging" for which they try to criticize others who utilize the Bible as their guidebook?

How is it different when a person who holds the Judeo-Christian Scriptures in high regard observes behavior and is able to simply determine if such behavior does or does not align with the principles found in them?

How do you deal with the influence of immoral or rebellious people around you?

How do you deal with it when these people take the form of false teachers hiding out and operating in the church?

Reread: 2 Peter 2:10

On whom is God particularly hard?

What attitudes and actions seem to characterize these people on whom God is particularly hard?

Why do you think these actions and attitudes seem to quite often go hand in hand?

Reread: 2 Peter 2:11

In what practice do the angels dare not do that false teachers unwisely engage?

Reread: 2 Peter 2:10-19

Here we find that the people about whom God is particularly displeased are also referenced as "false teachers." In 2 Peter 2:10-15 we find listed many of the qualities and traits that characterize such people. Please list them.

    1.

    2.

    3.

    4.

    5.

    6.

    7.

    8.

    9.

10.

11.

12.

13.

14.

15.

16.

17.

18.

19.

20.

21.

22.

23.

24.

25.

26.

27.

28.

29.

30.

31. .

32.

Reread: 2 Peter 2:14

It is most interesting that in this verse Peter, a fisherman by trade, uses a fishing term. The Greek word he uses is *delaezo,* which is translated as "lure, luring, or beguiling" in various versions of the Bible. In the fishing world it literally means "bait." What insight might we gain from this?

What kind of "bait" do false teachers sometimes use with success?

If you enjoy the sport of fishing, what do you do when you have found a "bait" that seems to attract a lot of fish?

In what way do false teachers do the same? Please give an example.

Reread: 2 Peter 2:16

In what way did God rebuke Balaam?

Reread: 2 Peter 2:17

Note: In this verse Peter uses the imagery of a well or spring without water. This is in direct contrast to what he heard and we read from Jesus in:

John 4:13-14

John 7:38

Why do you think Peter used this particular picture to get across his point?

What did Peter say is reserved for false teachers?

Reread: 2 Peter 2:18

How did and do false teachers attempt to affect others?

Reread: 2 Peter 2:19

What do false teachers deceptively promise?

To what does God's Word tell us these false teachers are slaves?

To what is a person a slave?

Is it possible for this "slavery" to in any way be good? Please read the following verses as you construct your answer:

Mark 9:35

2 Peter 1:1

Romans 1:1-4

James 1:1

Titus 1:1

Philippians 1:1

1 Timothy 4:6

Please explain.

Reread: 2 Peter 2:20

Note: Here we see Peter using yet another term from the world of fishing. The word he uses is most often translated "entangled" or "tangled up." Understanding what this means to a person who is fishing, how might you apply it to the principle Peter is discussing? Please explain.

How can a person escape the corruption that is rampant in the world?

What is the difference between understanding Judeo-Christianity as a system and having a personal, life-giving and redeeming relationship with Jesus Christ?

Please read for more information about the position people find themselves in when they gain an intellectual understanding about God and His ways but fail to enter into a real and personal relationship with Him through His Son.

Hebrews 6:4-6

Hebrews 10:26-31

At this point it might also be helpful to review some of the Scriptural references that help us to understand that a person who has truly committed themselves to Jesus Christ is secure. Please read:

Isaiah 49:23

John 3:16

Ephesians 2:8-9

Romans 8:28-39

Hebrews 7:25

Romans 10:10

Romans 10:11

Ephesians 1:13

1 Corinthians 15:1-4

2 Corinthians 5:17

1 Thessalonians 5:8

2 Timothy 1:12

1 Peter 2:6

How are we assured of our salvation?

What part does God's Word play in our assurance?

Reread: 2 Peter 2:21

In what position do false teachers and those misled by them find themselves?

Reread: 2 Peter 2:22

How does God's Word describe a person who has knowingly, willfully and overtly decided to rebel against God's standard for life?

Note: Many people in the civilized world today have dogs and even pigs as pets. In fact, many people love these pets as we do our dog "Benny." However, in Scripture these animals are generally regarded as "unclean." They were often used as a symbol of a false teacher. See:

Proverbs 26:11

Exodus 11:7

Judges 7:5

Psalm 22:20

Psalm 59:6

Psalm 59:14

Matthew 7:6

Have you ever been tempted to return to a destructive activity or attitude? If so, how do you deal with the situation?

Note: Read Ephesians 6:10-18 for guidance.

Application Questions

What false teachings do you need to expose as untrue?

How can you expose false teachings while having a positive impact? (See Colossians 4:5-6 and Ephesians 4:29-30 for some tips.)

What steps will you take to remain faithful and strong while living in a corrupt world?

Close in Prayer

WEEK 13

FINAL WARNINGS AND ENCOURAGEMENT
2 PETER 3:1-18

Open in Prayer

Group Warm-Up Questions

When was the last time someone wrote you an encouraging letter or note?

With what sort of people do you find it hard to be patient?

Read: 2 Peter 3:1-18

Reread: 2 Peter 3:1

What two specific reasons did Peter cite for writing his two letters?

1.

2.

What stimulates you to wholesome thinking?

What discourages people from engaging in wholesome thinking?

Reread: 2 Peter 3:2

What two particular categories of knowledge did Peter want his readers to recall?

1.

2.

Why are these two types of things vitally important to one's growth, confidence and effectiveness as a follower of the Jewish Messiah?

Read:

Revelation 19:10

John 16:4

Matthew 28:20

Joshua 1:9

What additional insights do we gain from these verses?

Reread: 2 Peter 3:3

What things did Peter say would happen at some point in the future? There are at least three in this verse.

1.

2.

3.

When did he say this would happen?

Reread: 2 Peter 3:4

What did Peter say these scoffers would say at this point in time?

Do you hear people saying such things today? Please give an example.

Where do you think we now stand in terms of history?

How close do you think we are to the days Peter spoke of? Please explain.

Reread: 2 Peter 3:5

What do these scoffers forget?

Peter says these people do this "deliberately." Why do you think they make such an effort to forget the truth?

What impact does it have upon the life of a person who deliberately forgets the lessons of history and God's interaction with human beings?

Reread: 2 Peter 3:6-7

How did God destroy the ancient world?

In what way do we learn that God will someday destroy the world as we know it?

For what reason do we learn that God will destroy what we think of as the "modern day" world?

Read:

2 Peter 2:5

Genesis 6:5-6

Genesis 6:11-13

How is what we read in 2 Peter 3:6-7 similar to what happened in the days of Noah?

Why is it that so many people think they can live as they wish without personal and societal consequence?

Read:

Galatians 6:6-7

Proverbs 14:14

Proverbs 11:25

Proverbs 11:24

Proverbs 22:8

Luke 6:38

Job 4:8-9

Proverbs 1:24-31

James 3:17-18

Psalm 106:3-4

Hosea 10:12

Genesis 12:1-3

2 Corinthians 5:9-10

2 Corinthians 9:6

2 Chronicles 7:14

Psalm 1:1-3

What does God have to say about personal and corporate consequences?

How does the fact that the earth will one day be destroyed affect your daily life?

Reread: 2 Peter 3:8

What did Peter tell his readers to remember about time?

How does it make you feel to realize that God exists outside the construct of time?

Note: One must be careful with this verse as with all others to not take it out of context. It must be viewed in concert with the rest of Scripture to realize that it speaks of the nature of God and then in the next verse of His patience and love even in the presence of His objective holiness. It most decidedly **does not** speak of the age of the earth, Darwinism or evolution as some "scholars" with a limited understanding of the Scriptures, history, geology and archaeology purport.

For more on how to properly understand such things I again suggest that one review "How to Avoid Error" in the appendices of this book as well as the thousands of intensely erudite and scholarly scientific articles and videos at *creation.com*.

Reread: 2 Peter 3:9

Also read:

Numbers 14:18

Psalm 86:15

Romans 9:22-24

Isaiah 48:9

Joel 2:13

Nahum 1:3

Romans 2:4

Habakkuk 2:3

Why does God not immediately impose the deserved sentence from His judgement on the world?

Why do you think He is so patient?

Do you feel as if God has been too patient with some people? How and why?

Has God been patient with you? How so?

If there is any incongruity between how you feel regarding God's patience with you in comparison to other people, how do you explain it?

Speaking of patience, it may be possible for a person to inadvertently and unexpectedly reach the time in which God's patience comes to an end. Some people believe they will have and then take the time to "get right with God" right before their death. Besides the obvious fallacy and ineffectiveness of trying to fool God (See Galatians 6:7-8 again.) one never knows if they will have such an opportunity. Witness the case of Pokémon designer **Eric Medalle**. While I have no idea what his spiritual condition might have been, we do know how his life ended.

At 3:30 p.m. on March 22, 2016 Daniel Berthencourt of the Detroit Free Press reported in USA Today that Eric had been driving through a park one day with his one year old daughter in the back seat. As he drove down a wooded road a giant Douglas fir tree fell onto his car killing him immediately upon impact. He apparently never saw the tree coming and his daughter was unhurt.

What other situations can you think of when someone's life ends suddenly and without warning?

How can we be sure that we are certain of our position with God even if life is immediately and unexpectedly terminated?

How can we help those about whom we care be certain of their ultimate destiny?

Reread: 2 Peter 3:10

Note: This verse is most amazing in that it contains two concepts that span approximately 1,007 years. (I am here assuming 7 years for what is known as *The Great Tribulation* and 1,000 years for what is called *The Millennium*.) The first sentence relates to what is commonly known as the **"Rapture."** This is also referenced throughout Scripture in many places including:

John 14:1-3

Romans 8:19

1 Corinthians 1:7-8

1 Corinthians 15:1-53

1 Corinthians 16:22

Philippians 3:20-21

Colossians 3:4

1 Thessalonians 1:8-10

1 Thessalonians 2:19

1 Thessalonians 4:13-18

1 Thessalonians 5:9

1 Thessalonians 5:23

2 Thessalonians 2:1-3

1 Timothy 6:13-14

2 Timothy 2:12-13

Titus 2:12-13

Hebrews 9:28

James 5:7-9

1 Peter 1:7

1 Peter 1:13

1 John 2:28-3:2

Jude 21

Revelation 2:25

Revelation 3:10

The second concept is that of the **second coming** of Jesus culminating in a new heaven and a new earth.

Daniel 2:44-45

Daniel 7:9-14

Daniel 12:1-3

Zechariah 14:1-15

Matthew 13:41

Matthew 24:15-31

Matthew 26:64

Mark 13:14-27

Mark 14:62

Luke 21:25-28

Acts 1:9-11

Acts 3:19-21

2 Timothy 4:1-2

1 Thessalonians 3:13

2 Thessalonians 1:6-10

2 Thessalonians 2:8

2 Peter 3:1-14

Jude 14-15

Revelation 1:7

Revelation 19:11-20:6

Revelation 22:7 (This verse is also sometimes applied to the Rapture.)

Revelation 22:12

Revelation 22:20 (Like Revelation 22:7, this verse is also sometimes applied to the Rapture.)

The subject of prophecy is found throughout the Judeo Christian Scriptures. Yet many ministers and denominations today seem to fear it. Perhaps this is from primarily desiring to see people grow in their relationship to God or in other cases because of sketchy scholarship. Either way, it can deprive one of a full understanding of God's character and His absolute objective standards. This difficulty is similar to that faced by people who concentrate only on the New Testament without grounding in the Old. In relationship to this subject, consider this:

1. In the whole of Scripture:

    • There are 8,362 predictive verses.

    • 1,817 predictions about the future are made.

    • The predictions made cover 737 separate matters.

    • Every prediction made has come true at the foreseen time.

    • There are yet some prophecies still to be fulfilled at the right time.

2. In Revelation, the last book of the Bible:

    • There are 404 verses.

    • Over 800 allusions are made to the Old Testament and the concepts and truth found therein.

3. In relationship to Jesus Christ, aka Yeshua Ha-Maschiach, the Jewish Messiah:

    • There are over 300 references to His first coming in the Old Testament.

    • There are over 1,845 references to His second coming and future rule on earth in the Old and New Testaments combined.

- The references to His second coming and rule on earth are prominent in 17 books of the Tanakh (what Jews call the Old Testament).

- In the New Testament the concepts of His return and subsequent rule are mentioned in 23 of 27 books.

Reread: 2 Peter 3:10

Also read:

Matthew 24:37-44

1 Thessalonians 5:1-3

Isaiah 65:17

How will the day come when Jesus returns to take those who belong to Him home?

What will happen on the subsequent day of judgement and thereafter?

For further study on these subjects I might suggest one access some of the excellent resources available including:

1. Several books, DVD and CD series produced by David Jeremiah and his *Turning Point* ministry.

2. The books, CDs, and workbooks produced by Koinonia House founded by Dr. Charles Missler.

3. The 590 page inductive Bible Study guide entitled *Dynamic Studies in Revelation.*

Note: The only word of caution one might adhere to in engaging in any such study is to be sure that what they are reading and hearing is consistent with what we find in God's inerrant Word: the Bible. To that end we should keep Acts 17:11 in mind which says, "The Bereans were more noble than these others. They searched the Scriptures (Old Testament in their case) every day to see if what Paul said was true."

Realize for an instant what this means. Paul was perhaps the most intelligent, well-read, and highly educated man of his time. The early believers were told in God's Word itself to check up even on Paul as well as others. Many of these believers were very intelligent, though none likely as smart as Paul, but they were being told to check up on this amazing intellectual giant. The crucible for what he, and what anyone else said, no matter how intelligent and convincing they may be, is the written Word of God which is available to us today as the Bible.

Even with all this knowledge why is it so easy for people to spend little time looking forward to the new heaven and earth?

Reread: 2 Peter 3:11-12

Also read:

Malachi 4:1

Joel 2:10

Matthew 24:29

Mark 13:24-25

Psalm 46:6

Micah 1:4

Knowing how history to come will turn out, what kind of lives ought we to be living now?

Reread: 2 Peter 3:13

Also read:

Isaiah 65:17

Isaiah 66:22

Revelation 21:1

To what are we to be looking forward?

What will characterize this construct? With what will the component parts be filled?

Reread: 2 Peter 3:14 and 2 Peter 3:11

What qualities should be overtly evident in the lives of believers, especially as they understand the reality of time and the future? Please list them.

1.

2.

3.

4.

5.

6.

The Sad End of David Cassidy

For those who remember, David Cassidy was regarded by many as a "heartthrob" in the 1970's. He died on November 22, 2017 at the age of 67 from organ failure. This was reported in the news as having stemmed from his "ongoing battle with dementia." If organ failure as a result of dementia sounds a little suspicious you are not alone. Cassidy himself cited his long-term abuse of alcohol and marijuana. His old friend and singer Kim Carnes spoke of "intense conversations they shared accompanied by wine and *weed." However, the saddest words Cassidy ever spoke were his last as shared by his daughter, Katie Cassidy. Before closing his eyes in death he said "so much wasted time."*

Similarly, John Greenleaf Whittier famously wrote: "For all sad words of tongue and pen, the saddest are these, 'It might have been.'"

What can we do today to be sure our days are characterized by the admonitions of God's Word as summarized by Peter instead of those from David Cassidy and John Whittier?

Reread: 2 Peter 3:15

What do we find reiterated about God's patience in this verse?

Why does He extend it to us?

Reread: 2 Peter 3:16

Also read:

2 Timothy 4:3-4

Romans 16:17-20

1 Timothy 4:1

2 Corinthians 11:14-15

2 Timothy 2:15

1 Timothy 6:3-5

2 Peter 2:1

Acts 17:11

Galatians 1:6-9

Revelation 22:18-19

What have some people done with Paul's letters as well as with the rest of Scripture?

How does Peter characterize these people?

What is the final result of twisting God's Word to one's own purposes in the lives of those who do it?

How can we be sure that we faithfully read, study, understand and apply God's Word to our lives today?

Read:

Hebrews 10:25

1 Thessalonians 5:16-21

2 Timothy 3:16-17

John 14:26

1 John 2:27

What role does prayer, Bible study itself, the Holy Spirit, and other believers play in this process? Please explain.

Reread: 2 Peter 3:17

About what did Peter say believers must be on guard?

As previously established, he is not worried about people losing their salvation, but he is very worried about something else. How would you describe the subject of his worry?

What happens in a person's life when they fail to avail themselves of the many resources God has provided them (as noted succinctly in the discussion above about 2 Peter 3:16)?

How effective is a person for God and good when they become confused?

Read: Revelation 3:14-17

Does such a person become like some of the people in Laodicea? How so?

Read: Matthew 28:20

What charge do all believers have from Jesus Christ?

What promise do all people who have committed themselves to Jesus Christ have?

Reread: 2 Peter 3:18

With what final admonition does Peter end his two famous letters?

With what additional final statement regarding Jesus Christ does Peter finish?

What is due to Jesus both now and forever?

How does it help a person to remember this on an ongoing basis?

Application Questions

To whom can you write a card, note, or letter of encouragement this week?

What will you do this week to stimulate wholesome thinking?

What change can you make in your routine to reflect your confident hope and assurance of the return of Jesus Christ?

Close in Prayer

APPENDIX 1

HOW TO AVOID ERROR
(PARTIALLY EXCERPTED FROM THE ROAD TO HOLOCAUST BY HAL LINDSEY)

1. The most important single principle in determining the true meaning of any doctrine of our faith is that we start with the clear statements of the Scriptures that specifically apply to it, and use those to interpret the parables, allegories and obscure passages. This allows Scripture to interpret Scripture. The Dominionists (and others seeking to bend Scripture to suit their purposes) frequently reverse this order, seeking to interpret the clear passages using obscure passages, parables and allegories.

2. The second most important principle is to consistently interpret by the literal, grammatical, historical method. This means the following:

   1. Each word should be interpreted in light of its normal, ordinary usage that was accepted in the times in which it was written.

   2. Each sentence should be interpreted according to the rules of grammar and syntax normally accepted when the document was written.

   3. Each passage should also be interpreted in light of its historical and cultural environment.

Most false doctrines and heresy of Church history can be traced to a failure to adhere to these principles. Church history is filled with examples of disasters and wrecked lives wrought by men failing to base their doctrine, faith, and practice upon these two principles.

The Reformation, more than anything else, was caused by an embracing of the literal, grammatical, and historical method of interpretation, and a discarding of the allegorical method. The allegorical system had veiled the Church's understanding of many vital truths for nearly a thousand years.

Note 1: It is important to note that this is how Jesus interpreted Scripture. He interpreted literally, grammatically, and recognized double reference in prophecy.

Note 2: It is likewise important that we view Scripture as a whole. Everything we read in God's Word is part of a cohesive, consistent, integrated message system. Every part of Scripture fits in perfectly with the whole of Scripture if we read, understand, and study it properly.

Note 3: Remember to **Appropriate the power of The Holy Spirit.**

Read: Luke 11:11-13   Read: I Timothy 4:15-16

Read: Luke 24:49   Read: II Peter 2:1

Read: John 7:38-39   Read: Mark 13:22

Read: John 14:14-17, 26

APPENDIX 2

UNDERSTANDING COMPOSITE PROBABILITY AND APPLYING IT TO THE JUDEO-CHRISTIAN SCRIPTURES

Before proceeding we might briefly reflect upon the reliability of the Judeo-Christian Scriptures. All honest researchers into their veracity have found that, as historical documents, they are without parallel. They are the most reliable and incontrovertibly accurate documents available in the world today. This has been the conclusion of all the erudite scholars and investigators who have taken the time to delve into this topic. For more information on this subject you may wish to read *The Case For Christ* by Lee Stroebel, *More Than a Carpenter* by Josh McDowell, and the *Evidence That Demands a Verdict* series, also by Josh McDowell. This is, of course, a very short list of the volumes available. A great deal of augmentative and corroborative material is available in such volume that if one were so inclined they might spend a lifetime in its study.

To better understand one of the ways the Creator of the Universe has validated His Word and the work and person of Jesus Christ, it is helpful to get a grasp on composite probability theory and its application to the Judeo-Christian Scriptures.

We are indebted to Peter W. Stoner, past chairman of the Department of Mathematics and Astronomy at Pasadena City College as well as to Dr. Robert C. Newman with his Ph.D. in astrophysics from Cornell University for the initial statistical work on this topic. Their joint efforts on composite probability theory were first published in the book *Science Speaks.*

Composite Probability Theory

If something has a 1 in 10 chance of occurring, that is easy for us to understand. It means that 10 percent of the time, the event will happen. However, when we calculate the probability of several different events occurring at the same time, the odds of that happening increase exponentially. This is the basic premise behind composite probability theory.

If two events have a 1 in 10 chance of happening, the chance that both of these events will occur is 1 in 10 x 10, or 1 in 100. To show this numerically this probability would be 1 in 10^2, with the superscript indicating how many tens are being multiplied. If we have 10^3, it means that we have a number of 1000. Thus 10^4 is equivalent to 10,000 and so on. This is referred to as 10 to the first power, 10 to the second power, 10 to the third power, and so on.

For example, let's assume that there are ten people in a room. If one of the ten is left handed and one of the ten has red hair, the probability that any one person in the room will be left handed and have red hair is one in one hundred.

We can apply this model to the prophecy revealed in the Bible to figure out the mathematical chances of Jesus' birth, life and death, in addition to many other events occurring in the New Testament by chance. To demonstrate this, we will consider eight prophecies about Jesus and assign a probability of them occurring individually by chance. To eliminate any disagreement, we will be much more limiting than is necessary. Furthermore, we will use the prophecies that are arguably the most unlikely to be fulfilled by chance. I think you will agree that in doing so, we are severely handicapping ourselves.

1. The first prophecy from Micah 5:2 says, "But you, O Bethlehem Ephrathah, are only a small village in Judah. Yet a ruler of Israel will come from you, one whose origins are from the distant past" (NLT). This prophecy tells us that the Messiah will be born in Bethlehem. What is the chance of that actually occurring? As we consider this, we also have to ask: What is the probability that anyone in the history of the world might be born in this obscure town? When we take into account all of the people who ever lived, this might conservatively be 1 in 200,000.

Amazingly, about 700 years after this prophecy was uttered it was fulfilled when Yeshua HaMaschiach (The Jewish Messiah), who we call Jesus, was born in exactly the place predicted. We see this in Luke 2:11 where it states "The Savior— yes, the Messiah, the Lord—has been born today in Bethlehem, the city of David!"

2. Let's move on to the second prophecy in Zechariah 9:9: "Rejoice greatly, O people of Zion! Shout in triumph, O people of Jerusalem! Look, your King is coming to you. He is righteous and victorious, yet He is humble, riding on a donkey---even on a donkey's colt" (NLT). For our purposes, we can assume the chance that the Messiah (the King) riding into Jerusalem on a donkey might be 1 in 100. But, really, how many kings in the history of the world have actually done this?

The fulfillment of this particular prophecy 500 years later was so unnerving that Matthew, Mark, Luke and John all included it in their historical accounts.

Matthew recorded it as "Tell the people of Jerusalem, 'Look, your King is coming to you. He is humble, riding on a donkey— riding on a donkey's colt' " (Matthew 21:5 NLT).

This appears in John's writings as "The next day, the news that Jesus was on the way to Jerusalem swept through the city. A large crowd of Passover visitors took palm branches and went down the road to meet him. They shouted, "Praise God! Blessings on the one who comes in the name of the LORD! Hail to the King of Israel!" Jesus found a young donkey and rode on it, fulfilling the prophecy that said: "Don't be afraid, people of Jerusalem. Look, your King is coming, riding on a donkey's colt" (John 12:12–15 NLT).

3. The third prophecy is from Zechariah 11:12: "I said to them, 'If you like, give me my wages, whatever I am worth; but only if you want to.' So they counted out for my wages thirty pieces of silver" (NLT). What is the chance that someone would be betrayed and the price of that betrayal would be thirty pieces of silver? For our purposes, let's assume the chance that anyone in the history of the world would be betrayed for thirty pieces of silver might be 1 in 1,000.

As unlikely as it may have seemed on the surface, this prediction was fulfilled approximately 500 years later and was noted by Matthew with the language itself being eerily similar to what had been written so many years ago. The NLT shows this as "How much will you pay me to betray Jesus to you? And they gave him thirty pieces of silver." (Matthew 26:15) How shocking would it be if you found that someone predicted exactly what you were going to spend for your next dinner out 500 years ago?

4. The fourth prophecy comes from Zechariah 11:13: "And the Lord said to me, 'Throw it to the potter'---this magnificent sum at which they valued me! So I took the thirty coins and threw them to the potter in the Temple of the Lord" (NLT). Now we need to consider what the chances would be that a temple and a potter would be involved in someone's betrayal. For our statistical model, let's assume this is 1 in 100,000.

This prophecy and its fulfillment is a continuation and completion of the one immediately prior to it in which the exact amount of the bribe for the betrayal of the Jewish King was predicted, again 500 years before it occurred. Here we find predicted not only the betrayal and the exact payment, but the actual usage of the funds. Matthew records fulfillment of this whole process as "I have sinned," he declared, "for I have betrayed an innocent man." "What do we care?" they retorted. "That's your problem." Then Judas threw the silver coins down in the Temple and went out and hanged himself. The leading priests picked up the coins. "It wouldn't be right to put this money in the Temple treasury," they said, "since it was payment for murder." After some discussion they finally decided to buy the potter's field, and they made it into a cemetery for foreigners (Matthew 27:4-7 NLT).

5. The fifth prophecy in Zechariah 13:6 reads: "And one shall say unto him, What are these wounds in thine hands? Then he shall answer, Those with which I was wounded in the house of my friends" (KJV). The question here is, "How many people in the history of the world have died with wounds in their hands?" I believe we can safely assume the chance of any person dying with wounds in his or her hands is somewhat greater than 1 in 1,000.

Again, 500 years later we see this specific prophecy fulfilled and the evidence viewed by Jesus's disciples in John 20:20 where it says "As he spoke, he showed them the wounds in his hands and his side. They were filled with joy when they saw the Lord" (NLT)!

6. The sixth prophecy in Isaiah 53:7 states, "He was oppressed and treated harshly, yet he never said a word. He was led like a lamb to the slaughter. And as a sheep is silent before the shearers, he did not open his mouth" (NLT). This raises a particularly tough question. How many people in the history of the world can we imagine being put on trial, knowing they were innocent, without making one statement in their defense? For our statistical model, let's say this is 1 in 1,000, although it is pretty hard to imagine.

In this case, approximately 700 years passed between the time the prediction was made and we see it fulfilled in Mark 15:3-5. There it is recorded as "Then the leading priests kept accusing him of many crimes, and Pilate asked him, "Aren't you going to answer them? What about all these charges they are bringing against you?" But Jesus said nothing, much to Pilate's surprise" (NLT).

7. Moving on to the seventh prophecy, Isaiah 53:9 says "He had done no wrong and had never deceived anyone. But he was buried like a criminal; he was put in a rich man's grave" (NLT). Here we need to consider how many people, out of all the good individuals in the world who have died, have died a criminal's death and been buried in a rich person's grave. These people died out of place. (Some might also infer that they were buried out of place, though that is not necessarily true.) Let's assume the chance of a good person dying as a criminal and being buried with the rich is about 1 in 1,000.

Again we find that 700 years passed between the prediction of this event and the actual occurrence. Again, this event was so momentous that it was recorded by Matthew, Mark, Luke and John. Astonishingly, we find that he was placed in the tomb by not just one person of wealth, but by two. Joseph of Arimathea and Nicodemus, two of the wealthiest men in the region, worked together and laid the body in Joseph's own tomb. Matthew 27:60, speaking of Joseph of Arimathea's part in entombing Jesus' body says "He placed it in his own new tomb, which had been carved out of the rock. Then he rolled a great stone across the entrance and left" (NLT).

8. The eighth and final prophecy is from Psalm 22:16: "My enemies surround me like a pack of dogs; an evil gang closes in on me. They have pierced my hands and feet" (NLT). Remember this passage and all the other prophetic references to the crucifixion were written before this form of execution was invented. However, for our purposes, we just need to consider the probability of someone in the history of the world being executed by crucifixion. Certainly, Jesus wasn't the only person killed by being crucified. We will say that the chances of a person dying from this specific form of execution to be at 1 in 10,000.

Here we might note that Psalm 22 was penned by King David approximately 1000 years prior to the birth of Jesus. The word "crucifixion" and its derivatives had not yet been coined, but we see the process described in detail. Again, because of the import of this event it is recorded by each of the Gospel writers. In Mark 16:6 we see the fulfillment of the ancient prophecy and more where we read "Don't be alarmed. You are looking for Jesus of Nazareth, who was crucified. He isn't here! He is risen from the dead! Look, this is where they laid his body" (NLT).

Calculating the Results

To determine the chance that all these things would happen to the same person by chance, we simply need to multiply the fraction of each of the eight probabilities. When we do, we get a chance of 1 in 10^{28}. In other words, the probability is 1 in 10,000,000,000,000,000,000,000,000,000.

Would you bet against these odds?

Unfortunately, there is another blow coming for those who do not believe the Bible is true or Jesus is who He said He was. There are not just eight prophecies of this nature in the Bible that were fulfilled in Jesus Christ------there are *more than three hundred* such prophecies in the Old Testament. The prophecies we looked at were just the ones that we could *most easily* show fulfilled.

If we deal with only forty-eight prophecies about Jesus, based on the above numbers, the chance that Jesus is not who He said He was or the Bible is not true is 1 in 10^{168}. This is a larger number than most of us can grasp (though you may want to try to write it sometime). To give you some perspective on just how big this number is, consider these statistics from the book *Science Speaks* by Peter Stoner:

- If the state of Texas were buried in silver dollars two feet deep, it would be covered by 10^{17} silver dollars.

- In the history of the world, only 10^{11} people have supposedly ever lived. (I don't know who counted this.)

- There are 10^{17} seconds in 1 billion years.

- Scientists tell us that there are 10^{66} atoms in the universe and 10^{80} particles in the universe.

- Looking at just forty-eight prophecies out of more than three hundred, there is only a 1 in 10^{168} chance of Jesus not being who He said He was or of the Bible being wrong.

In probability theory, the threshold for an occurrence being absurd---translate that as "impossible"---is only 10^{50}. No thinking person who understands these probabilities can deny the reality of our faith or the Bible based on intellect. Every person who has set out to disprove the Judeo-Christian Scriptures on an empirical basis has ended up proving the Bible's authenticity and has, in most cases, become a believer.

These facts are more certain than any others in the world. However, not everyone who has come to realize the reliability and reality of these documents has become a believer. These intelligent people who understand the statistical impossibility that Jesus was not who He claimed to be and who yet do not make a decision for Christ are not senseless; they generally just have other issues. They allow these issues to stop them from enjoying the many experiential benefits that God offers them through His Word and the dynamic relationship they could have with Him, not to mention longer-term benefits. These people, of course, deserve love and prayer, because this is not just a matter of the intellect. If it were, every intelligent inquirer would be a believer. Rather, it is very much a matter of the heart, the emotions, and the spirit.

The truth of this statement was brought home to me in one very poignant situation. In this case, someone very near and dear to me said, "But Dad, this could have been anybody." No, this could not have been just anybody. The chance these prophecies could have been fulfilled in one person is so remote as to be absurd. That is impossible. Only one person in human history fulfilled these prophecies and that person is Jesus Christ. To claim otherwise is not intelligent, it is not smart, it is not well-considered, and it is not honest. It may be emotionally satisfying, but in all other respects it is self-delusional.